CRIMES PAST

Glasgow's Crimes of the Century

Robert Jeffrey

BLACK & WHITE PUBLISHING

First published 2006
by Black & White Publishing Ltd,
99 Giles Street, Edinburgh EH6 6BZ

ISBN 13   9 781845 020903
ISBN 10   1 84502 090 1

A CIP catalogue record for this book is available from the British Library.

Book designed by Creative Link, North Berwick
Printed and bound in Poland
www.polskabook.pl

To purchase copies of the photographs in *Crimes Past*, please
contact Newsquest Photo Sales Department on 0141 302 7000

Acknowledgements

I would like to acknowledge the work of Ian Watson, Malcolm Beaton, Jim McNeish, and Tony Murray of Newsquest in the production of this book and thank them for their highly professional assistance. I would also like to thank Walter Norval and his daughter Rita for their help.

In the early days of newspapers, the photographers usually had a darkroom close to the news desk. The smell of developers and fixers and the pungent odour from hot glossy prints in the drying cabinet mingled with the cigarette smoke and occasional whisky fumes of the newsroom, where the reporters and subeditors toiled. It was not the practice then to give photographers bylines and some of their best images appeared anonymously. Many didn't even add their name to the back of the prints destined for the archive. Their work remained unacknowledged. Many of the images in this book are by unnamed staff photographers. Others we know are from the lenses of such respected 'snappers' as Harry Moyes, Duncan Stewart, Arthur Kinloch, Gordon Terris, John Young, Stuart Paterson, James Miller, Duncan Dingsdale, Eddie Jones, Robert Patterson, Chris James, Robin Gray and Ian Waldie. To all who took the pictures, named and unnamed, my thanks and admiration for their work.

By the same author:

Glasgow Crimefighter

(with Les Brown)

Blood on the Streets

Glasgow's Godfather

Gangland Glasgow

Glasgow's Hard Men

The Wee Book of Glasgow

The Wee Book of the Clyde

Images of Glasgow

Scotland's Sporting Heroes

The Herald Book of the Clyde

Doon the Watter

Clydeside, People and Places

(all with Ian Watson)

Contents

Behind bars – this is a situation that is, sadly, too familiar to many Glaswegians. A watery daylight struggles through the bars of a small window, the harsh electric light bounces off the white painted walls and a prisoner tries to make the best of it, reading to while away the long hours, or in some cases, years of incarceration. This was a typical Barlinnie cell photographed in 1981.

CHAPTER ONE

City with a Past — and a Future

There is no denying it – Glasgow is a city with a past, a city with 'form' as they say in the courts, in the pubs and on the streets of this remarkable place. This sometimes-desperate past belongs to a city of razor men, gangs, drug wars, infamous murderers and violence in dark streets and schemes – places often scarred by poverty and substandard housing. It has been making headlines for these reasons for more than a hundred years. It is as much a fact as the more palatable aspects of the city's reputation – the humour and sense of community found in the unlikeliest areas, the admirable renaissance of culture, visual arts, dance, music, both popular and classical, and cutting-edge architecture – that, in recent years, has made the city something of a wonder of western Europe.

Today Glasgow is a proud place of pavement cafes, galleries, theatres and restaurants, with internationally known chefs, labouring under the weight of critical accolades that attract tourists by the hundreds of thousands. The city does not disappoint them. And it is getting better. But the past is the past. It cannot be swept away, pushed into some forgotten folk memory or diminished by wilful disregard of the facts. The violence that is such a dramatic part of the Glasgow story cannot be tossed into a convenient drawer or file labelled 'history' and ignored. Apart from anything else, there are lessons to be learned by the new breed of crime fighters.

A study of crime in Glasgow down the years, from scandals of infamous women accused of murder, like Madeleine Smith and Jessie McLachlan, on to the Penny Mob of the early twentieth century, the sectarian gangs of the thirties and the drug-fuelled feuds of today, underlines one sombre fact. The city's story contains tales of many gangbusters, and many gangbusting initiatives by concerned citizens, legendary Chief Constables, famous social workers and preachers yet one thing has to be faced – the gangs are far from 'bust'. Indeed it is shocking that, in 2006, the London-based *Sunday Times* could write about a booze and blade culture that has made Scotland 'the most violent country in the developed world'. And no one could argue that Glasgow is not the crime capital of Scotland. A daily reading of the papers in these early days of the twenty-first century confirms that gangs still run wild and there remain areas where you take your life in your hands with a visit to the wrong pub or if you make a wrong remark in certain company. This continuing underbelly of violence is part of a cycle. Fighting crime in Glasgow can involve one step forward and two back. Historian John Prebble once called Glasgow 'a bold and defiant city' and remarked that its 'brawling, questioning people' are its majesty. The observation is still pertinent.

The cyclical nature of crime on the streets of this city is truly dispiriting. A study of what went on and what goes on shows that clearly. Chief Constables like Percy Sillitoe, David McNee, John Orr and others have had their successes – mostly when they were allowed the money to throw decent resources at the problem. But inevitably the strains on the police, traffic control, the high murder rate, burglary, vandalism and other crimes, less spectacular than gangs and drugs, mean that the eye comes off the ball after a time and the bad guys begin to come to the fore again. But one lesson of history is that short-term initiatives can work wonders. The work of such legendary ministers of the Kirk, like Warnes and Murray in Bridgeton in the early 1930s and Cameron Peddie in the Gorbals in the fifties, was for a time remarkably successful in partially curbing young, violent gangs – as was the controversial Easterhouse Project in the late sixties. It is interesting that Conservatives on the city council at that time shamefully attacked one of the leading lights of the project, the singer Frankie Vaughan, a long-term worker for boys' clubs, as something of a glory seeker and generally tried to do the work of the initiative down. But the police's

At least in Barlinnie the bed is well made, the cell is heated and three meals a day are guaranteed. Life outside could, on occasion, be harsher in some respects than that inside. In the thirties and forties, youngsters running with the street gangs would often call a sojourn in the Bar-L a holiday.
This picture of a Gorbals slum taken in the sixties shows why. A family of seven lived in this single room. The baby (six days old) slept in a basket. There were no cooking facilities, no water and only one light. The rent was thirty-nine shillings a week.

The exteriors of slums were equally dispiriting. This backcourt scene was shot in 1963 as two women climbed the crumbling stairs to homes that they tried to keep as clean and well kept as was possible in such dire surroundings.

To the Glaswegian, prison these days simply means the Bar-L (or one of the less rigorous establishments in the surrounding countryside considered more suitable for the less violent, dangerous or difficult prisoners). But many thousands lived behind the huge walls of Duke Street Prison, just a few hundred yards from George Square and almost in the shadow of the cathedral. Some also died on the prison's gallows. From around 1875, it was a place of execution where the condemned died in private. Previously, public hangings took place in Glasgow Green near the Saltmarket. This picture was used in the old *Bulletin* newspaper in 1935.

own statistics on the violence of the time, released many years later, showed that, for a spell at least, the figures for knife- and weapon-carrying, assaults and gang fights fell when the Easterhouse Project was making headlines and those in favour of it and those agin it were filling the airwaves and the letters pages of the newspapers.

The Easterhouse Project was, like most of such schemes, designed to alleviate the effects of that old, but true, cliché that 'the devil makes work for idle hands'. The Project provided premises for discos and meetings, encouraged the laying down of weapons and tried to get young tearaways to resolve their differences in decent surroundings, in the warmth and comfort of youth club premises and away from the cold, dark streets of a council scheme that, till then, had had little to offer potential teen gangsters with time on their hands and looking for trouble. In a similar vein, many years before, Warnes and Murray had started what was to become the Churches' League for amateur footballers and also encouraged boys to visit the countryside on outings to climb the cliffs of the Whangie on the road to Drymen and Loch Lomond and to knock lumps out of each other on the football field rather than in the back streets.

Inside, the Bar-L was a grim place but the photographers who were allowed to visit it often captured striking images. Here, in 1990, two officers are silhouetted against the bars as they walk with their sniffer dogs. Stuart McCall handled Jack and Stephen Wheeler handled Digger.

Duke Street Prison was demolished at the end of the fifties. Here a press party, including some well-kent city faces, are shown the trap in the execution block. They react with interest rather than horror.

Sir Percy Sillitoe came to prominence in 1931 when he led the police's gangbusting efforts in Sheffield. Glasgow had a similar problem with gangs and the city fathers invited him north. As Chief Constable, he had periods of great success with a philosophy that met violence with violence. But 'The Captain' or 'The Big Fella' as he was called was not simply a hard-man cop – he pioneered underwater squads and radio cars and was an innovative thinker.

For some bizarre reason, swords have always been something of a weapon of choice in the city. After the Second World War, some tearaways even carried them hidden in the leg shields of Italian motor scooters. But, as this *Evening Times* cutting shows, the hooligans were even more inventive in the 1930s – a swordfish's spear as a weapon in Bridgeton!

To some of its regular visitors, the big house in the east end was known as the Barlinnie Hotel. Here is the bill of fare for one summer day in the eighties. Traditionalists will note porridge being given its place, though in 2006 it is coming off the menu in some of the country's HMPs, to be replaced by suburban favourites like cornflakes!

A legacy left by Sillitoe was his invention of the black-and-white checked ribbon on police headgear. Making law officers instantly recognisable, it was taken up by many forces round the world. Here two officers use the novelty of in-car radio in what the original caption called 'the day and night war against crime'.

Some of the police work of the gangbusters was a bit more robust. Percy Sillitoe for example, was a bit of a believer in that old rugby axiom 'retaliate first'. Brought from Sheffield to Glasgow in the thirties to curb growing gang violence, particularly between the Billy Boys and their sectarian enemies the Norman Conks, he recruited the biggest and strongest constables in the force to form an elite squad, nicknamed the 'Untouchables'. These were the toughest, most aggressive men in the blue uniform and they used undercover cops to find the location and timing of gang fights, often Glasgow Green or Rutherglen Bridge, and fearlessly waded into the gangs with truncheons and fists. They soon won the respect of the city's hard men who quickly learned that the police were now no easy touch. Nowadays, such methods would, of course, run into conflict with the politically correct brigade

but, in their day, they worked. Indeed, after the Second World War, during one of the periodic outbreaks of gang violence, Sir Percy's son wrote from England to the *Glasgow Herald*, later called simply *The Herald,* pointing out his father's successes and remarking that, if the police were allowed to continue to use his methods these days, the city might be a safer place.

The files of *The Herald* and *Evening Times* are a prime source for anyone researching crime in this sometimes-benighted city. The evocative, historic photographs in this book mostly come from the remarkable collection of around four million images of the city and its citizens now held in the Mitchell Library. Stored in time-worn brown envelopes, these photographs are often tattered and yellowing and the captions on the back of the prints are usually scrawled in pencil by photographers

One of those who took on the difficult task of following in Sillitoe's footsteps as Chief Constable was Sir James Robertson. He had a pretty successful watch with methods rather different from Sillitoe and his tough squad of elite cops known as the 'Untouchables'. Robertson had a lifelong interest in youth and, when he retired in 1971, Joe Beattie, one of the most respected and best-remembered detectives in the city could say, 'He was a gentleman through and through. Sometimes I thought he was too nice to be a chief constable. He was too humane.'

Down the years, the city has been lucky with a succession of memorable Chiefs. Sir David McNee succeeded Robertson. He had worked as a constable in Partick and Anderston and had a classic progression to the top job. After leaving Glasgow in 1977, he was Commissioner of the Met for five years. Glaswegians like nicknames for cops and robbers and Sir David was known as 'The Hammer' for the way he tackled illegal money lenders. Being a policeman on the streets in this city is hard. The faces around Sir David in this 1977 long-service ceremony have seen it all.

The flavour of a night patrol in winter is caught in this shot of the crew of Echo Mike 3 near Glasgow Cross in 1979. The officers are Sandy Forsyth (left) and Eddie Mulgrew.

who worked, decade after decade, often using primitive equipment, to produce an irreplaceable pictorial record of the city on the banks of the Clyde, including the ugly side of life.

There is also shelf after shelf of heavy, dusty bound volumes of the newspapers themselves – now mostly converted to searchable microfilm – and they chronicle more than gang fighting, more than the razor-slashings and lowlife crimes of the past. As well as the doings of the Godfathers like Walter Norval and Arthur Thompson and the battles of the infamous gangs, there are intriguing tales of individual murders most foul. Violent, mysterious deaths were not confined to the squalor of the old Gorbals or the sink schemes or tenements of the east end – the city also has a fascinating history of murders that have become legendary, including some in the douce streets of the old cobbled west end.

Sadly there are shocking tales of injustice too – as demonstrated by the cases of Paddy Meehan and Oscar Slater and the long-running wrong meted out to big TC Campbell and Joe Steele, wrongly imprisoned for the Ice-Cream Wars murders. There are deep unsolved mysteries too and none is more intriguing than the search for the killer the press labelled Bible John.

Yes, this past of Glasgow is a curious thing – a rich mixture of backstreet thugs, Godfathers and violent gang leaders contrasted with men like 'Gentle' Johnny Ramensky, the cracksman who, during the Second World War, risked his life blowing German safes behind the lines in search of secret plans and who then came home to take up his old life of opening the safes of banks and businesses in search of unearned cash. The city has also been the scene of several infamous trials like that of mass murderer Peter Manuel. The journey through the years from poisoner Dr Edward Pritchard – known as the 'human crocodile' he became the last man to be publicly hanged in Glasgow – to such as Paul Ferris, Tam McGraw and the Thompsons, Arthur Senior and Junior, by way of scores of shocking crimes of all sorts, is as fascinating as anything in the annals of crime. This is a photograph album of that journey.

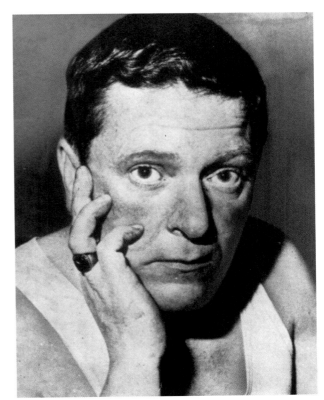

A pensive Paddy Meehan, victim of one of Glasgow's most horrific miscarriages of justice. He wasn't the only person to be imprisoned for a murder he did not commit – Meehan was preceded by Jessie McLachlan and Oscar Slater in the annals of injustice.

The Last Godfather, Arthur Thompson Sr, wrote himself into the violent history of the city leading a motley collection of enforcers and hard men. He survived several assassination attempts and died in his bed. Powerful and usually smartly dressed – to reinforce his claim to merely be a 'retired businessman' – he was a cold-eyed figure who exuded menace in any company.

Thompson and Johnny Ramensky may have shared the same criminal world but they were worlds apart in temperament. 'Gentle' Johnny, as he was known, spent much of his life behind bars as a result of his safe-breaking skills. But, as his nickname suggests, he was not a violent man and, when collared, went quietly and took his 'porridge' like a man. During the Second World War, he did brave and sterling service for his country, being parachuted behind German lines and breaking safes in search of secret plans. Here he enjoys a brief moment at his own fireside.

Jimmy Boyle is one of the most controversial figures in Glasgow's criminal history. Caged in Peterhead, he reacted like an animal. Moved to the Barlinnie Special Unit, he, along with writer Hugh Collins, became one of its most remarkable success stories. But sections of the public found the story of this murderer's redemption and transformation to successful artist, Rolls Royce owner and wine buff hard to take. However, the moment you are released from years in jail is like no other. This is Boyle leaving Saughton in 1982.

Perhaps the most famous journalist the city has produced, Jack House, here in George Square in the eighties, loved the city and was hugely knowledgeable about its history and its people. He never missed an opportunity to 'sell' the virtues of Glasgow, especially over Edinburgh, to anyone who would listen. But he was no stranger to the dark side of the place. In his early days as a reporter, he frequented the courts and, later in his career, wrote the remarkable book *Square Mile of Murder*. In it, he delved in detail into four of the most momentous crimes in these parts – the Madeleine Smith case, the Jessie McLachlan trial, the trial of the poisoner Dr Edward William Pritchard and the wrongful imprisonment of Oscar Slater.

CHAPTER TWO

Poison, Passion, Stained Glass and a Meat Cleaver

Sadly, but indisputably, the main thrust of the old reputation of Glasgow, anywhere crime is of interest, is a variation of the *No Mean City* tale – of unemployed men living by day in tenement hovels and coming out at night to fuel violence with hours spent in spit and sawdust pubs. Alexander McArthur and H. Kingsley Long's novel of life in the Gorbals was much criticised at the time for being as inaccurate as it was damaging to the city's image. Not so. The newspaper files tell of dozens of reporters sent to the Gorbals to interview people who lived through the dark days of the early thirties. And the scribes came back with a verdict that the famous novel's picture of life in the old Gorbals gangland, although a little dramatised, was not far from the truth.

But Glasgow has many faces. A few miles away from the old Gorbals slums, on the north bank of the river, lies the genteel west end with its famous 'wally' closes with their beautiful tiling and stained glass. Even closer stand impressive city-centre town houses, such as those around Blythswood Square.

Here, at the turn of the twentieth century, long before the slums and the gangs were grabbing headlines, crimes of a different style were afoot. Expensive curtains and blinds hung from the windows, valuable paintings adorned the walls, the furniture was dark and polished, maids and butlers went about their work, all of this out of sight of the well-dressed denizens of the area, seeing to their lawful business on foot or in the horse-drawn carriages that rattled along the cobbled streets. This was life in the west end and areas such as Dennistoun where society had built its cosy nests. But murder is not exclusive to the slums. In gas-lit Glasgow, crimes of greed and high passion were providing the news for the journals of the day and themes for books galore.

The most famous of the many books on the old crimes in the genteel, well-heeled parts of the city is Jack House's *Square Mile of Murder*. House, possibly the city's most famous journalist, told the story of notorious murders committed within a mile or so of the city centre around the end of the

Blythswood Square in August 1962. Office workers dot the grass as they seek to top up their tans. Away from the sunshine, the square had a more sinister side. For a time after dark, it was a frequent cruising place for prostitutes looking for city-centre business. Back in 1855, it was the home of Madeleine Smith and her family and it was from here that she passed a cup or two of cocoa to Pierre Emile L'Angelier, once her 'sweet pet', who was now surplus to requirements. As a consequence, the cocoa was topped up with a neat little dose of poison.

nineteenth century and the early days of the twentieth century. If, worldwide, Glasgow is a byword for gangs and razor-slashing, the likes of Madeleine Smith, who was accused of lacing her lover's late-night cocoa with a little touch of arsenic, have an equally international notoriety. Madeleine escaped the gallows on a dodgy not proven verdict, though later in life, having gone to America, she was said by no less than Somerset Maugham to have admitted killing Pierre Emile L'Angelier.

Oddly, America was the final resting place of another famous Glasgow woman charged with murder. Jessie McLachlan featured in a blood-soaked crime and also escaped the gallows. She eventually remarried and went to the New World where she died in Michigan of a heart attack on New Year's Day 1899. The murder of Jess McPherson, a friend of Jessie, in 1862 was a savage affair that brought a famous rhyme to mind:

> Lizzie Borden took an axe
> And gave her mother forty whacks.
> When she saw what she had done,
> She gave her father forty-one.

This sketch of Madeleine Smith captures the strong character of a woman who was ruthless and calculating as well as romantic. Her appearance and the deadly nature of the murder charge against her caused huge crowds to gather in the attempt to get a glimpse of the accused on her way into court.

Two of the ingredients of one of the world's great romantic crime mysteries – a letter from Madeleine Smith to Pierre L'Angelier and a bottle of arsenic from Currie, the apothecary in Sauchiehall Street. The poison, according to Madeleine, was for cosmetic use but there is no doubt some found its way into Pierre's cocoa.

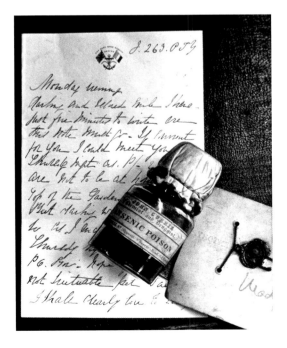

LOCAL NAMESTAMP, TYPE D1.
RECORDED IN BLUE AS A
BACKSTAMP 1854 — 1856 AND
IN BLACK AS A CANCELLATION
1856 — 1858.

Madeleine Smith and her 'sweet pet' conducted much of their romance through letters. This one was addressed to Emile at his Bothwell Street business where he worked as a seedsman.

This is the Blythswood Square window through which Madeleine Smith passed the poisoned cocoa.

M. P. E. L'ANGELEIR

The victim L'Angelier claimed to be French with links to the nobility but, in reality, he came from the Channel Islands. He caught the eye of Madeleine Smith and her sister Bessie as they took the air in Sauchiehall Street on mild nights. The twirling moustache and the fancy waistcoats gave him a dashing air but contemporary reports suggest that Pierre Emile was, like Madeleine herself, a touch on the plump side.

The Madeleine Smith affair has a fascination for writers – it has spawned at least four books, four plays (including one for television) and a film. After the success of *Square Mile of Murder*, which is still in print, visiting celebrities turned to Jack House for their info. Here he shows actress Ann Todd the scene of the crime. Madeleine died in America where she is said to have admitted her guilt and her luck at the not proven verdict. For years, aficionados of the case would visit the old Ramshorn Kirkyard in Ingram Street where the remains of Emile were interred in the Stevenson lair.

Most people who examine the case now conclude that Jess's killer was a dreadful hypocrite known as 'Old Fleming' who lived in some style at 17 Sandyford Place, near Charing Cross. A seemingly pious west-end gentleman, in reality, although elderly, he had difficulty keeping his hands off both the female servants and the whisky bottle. One servant was Jessie McLachlan who had kept up a friendship with Jess McPherson. With his son away down the coast one weekend, Old Fleming, with the house to himself, got involved with Jess and Jessie in a night of drink and drugs that would not have been out of place in some Californian beach hangout in the twenty-first century. Jess died as the result of what looked like forty whacks with a meat cleaver. But this was Glasgow around 150 years ago and the law was of the opinion that a Kirk elder and respectable figure like Old Fleming could not be guilty of an axe murder. So Jessie went to jail and, by the time of

her eventual release, Old Fleming was dead. Her conviction was an injustice – something that scars Glasgow's history several times as this look into crimes past shows.

The Oscar Slater trial in 1909 shocked the respectable west end where appearances were of great importance. For a spell, the crime dominated the talk of the city. The victim, a rich elderly spinster called Marion Gilchrist who lived in a flat in West Princes Street, again not far from Charing Cross, epitomised such respectability. Miss Gilchrist's wealth was such that she had £3000 worth of jewellery stashed around her well-furnished flat, a huge sum for the time. The gems were hidden behind curtains, stuffed into the pockets of clothes in the wardrobe and in other random hidey-holes. As Christmas 1908 neared, a neighbour found her battered to death. The neighbour had also spotted an intruder leaving the scene of the crime.

This sad-eyed portrait is of Jessie McLachlan who was involved in an amazing murder trial in the 1860s that involved sex, drink, drugs and a meat cleaver! Convicted, she was spared the gallows and, on hearing she was not to be 'hangit', remarked, 'I am to be kept in jail a' my days.' In prison, she insisted on her innocence and shunned the company of her fellow prisoners. On release, she, like Madeleine Smith, moved to America where she died in 1899.

THE MAN WHO DID

Pious and cunning, this is the Kirk elder **Old Fleming** who most now believe killed servant girl **Jess McPherson** though **Jessie McLachlan** was convicted of the crime.

This is the meat cleaver which killed Jess McPherson who was found wallowing in blood. Her injuries were said to be from 'forty whacks' – an allusion to the 'Lizzie Borden' rhyme that was much remarked on at the time. It is now in the Strathclyde Police museum.

The police were called and the stitch-up that was to send the innocent Slater to jail for nineteen years had begun. Slater, a German Jew, was known to the police in Glasgow at the time as a gambler and jewel dealer. A 'tip-off' to the detectives investigating the murder said he had tried to sell a pawn ticket for a brooch and, although a brooch was one of the items missing from the old gentlewoman's home, the police were able to establish that this brooch was not the one that had been stolen. However, the city was hungry for the police to find the evil killer of Marion Gilchrist – the newspapers and citizens could talk of little else. Slater, who did not know the police were aware that the brooch was legitimately his, panicked and fled to New York on the *Lusitania* with his glamorous show-business mistress. The police, under almost intolerable pressure to make an arrest, came up with the theory that Slater had fled because of newspaper reports that seemed to suggest he resembled the man who had been seen running from the crime scene.

Oscar was arrested in America but returned, voluntarily, to face trial, no doubt convinced that, since he had nothing to do with the crime, he would quickly be cleared. A dodgy identification parade, which has gone into police history as a classic example of how not to do it, resulted in him being identified as the killer. There was really no evidence against him other than this spurious identification and, indeed, after the trial he turned out to have had a solid alibi. But the police, no doubt spurred on by the court of public opinion, persisted that the foreigner was guilty. He was sentenced to hang but, in what itself was something

of a mystery, was reprieved a few hours before the rope was due to be placed round his neck. He was to serve nineteen years in jail.

He had been behind bars for five years when, in 1914, the case took a dramatic turn. John Trench, a detective who had been part of the original investigation, claimed that Miss Gilchrist's maid had named the man seen near the flat as someone known to her and her mistress. But the police had ignored every other avenue in their desire to stitch-up Slater who, in their view, made a suitable scapegoat. Trench had been told at the time to keep the maid's observation to himself. When he eventually released this information, there was an inquiry. Those who follow such matters to this day will not be surprised that it was a whitewash. Indeed, Detective Trench, the honest cop, was dismissed from the force for 'passing information to an outsider'.

It is not surprising that an inquiry into police incompetence, or worse, turned into a charade. It is likewise not surprising that such a flawed case as the one that was presented against Slater produced investigative writers to help free him. William Roughead, a notable writer on criminal matters of the time, campaigned against the verdict for years, as did Sir Arthur Conan Doyle, who knew a thing or two about crime, and the novelist Andrew Lang, who wrote that, on the kind of evidence presented against poor Oscar Slater, 'a cat would scarcely be whipped for stealing cream'.

The Slater story touches a chord with the case of Paddy Meehan, who was also unjustly jailed for many years for a crime he didn't commit and only released after a huge campaign by writers and lawyers. But that was to lie many years ahead and will be dealt with later in this book.

Another legendary case that has similar overtones to Madeleine Smith and Slater is that of the poisoner Dr Edward William Pritchard. This infamous killer ended his life on the gallows at Glasgow Green on 28 July 1865. It is said that around 80,000 to 100,000 gathered to watch him be dispatched into eternity by William Calcraft, the infamous 'London Hangman'. Pritchard was known at the time as the 'human crocodile', a name derived from a popular poem of the era called 'The Prince of Poisoners'. The lines that stuck in the public memory from this ode, penned by one Alexander Allan, were:

> And men condemn the murderer to die.
> But, when a wretch in secret hate and guile,
> A foul cold-blooded human crocodile,
> Plots calmly on for months, from day to day,
> To take his fellow creature life away –
> (and that the wife that in his bosom lay) –
> Counts out the grains of poison it requires
> To do the deed his hellish heart desires.

Pritchard was a figure of considerable hate in the city when it was revealed that this dandified ladies' man and so-called doctor (his medical experience was suspect) had slowly poisoned his wife and mother-in-law and, while in the process of doing so, he had dallied sexually with his family's servant girl. There was talk of other murders as well. The tabloids of today would have had a field day with the 'human crocodile', a charlatan with an ego so big that he was in the habit of handing out postcards of himself to passers-by in the street. And what would modern hacks make of the accounts at the time that claimed he had his victim's coffin opened and kissed her goodbye with a tear in his eye? There aren't too many modern villains with that style. He was immaculately dressed for his hanging, even down to white gloves, of which he wore one, carrying the other in his hand.

Poison was much in fashion in the old days of crimes past and, Madeleine Smith apart, the most famous poisoner was Dr Edward Prichard who was executed on Glasgow Green in 1865 for the murder of his wife and his mother-in-law. It is said around 80,000 turned up to watch him die. He dressed well for the occasion, including white gloves. A womaniser and dandy, he reportedly asked for his wife's coffin to be opened at the funeral and kissed the corpse with a tear in his eye. Because of this, a poem of the time dubbed him 'the human crocodile'.

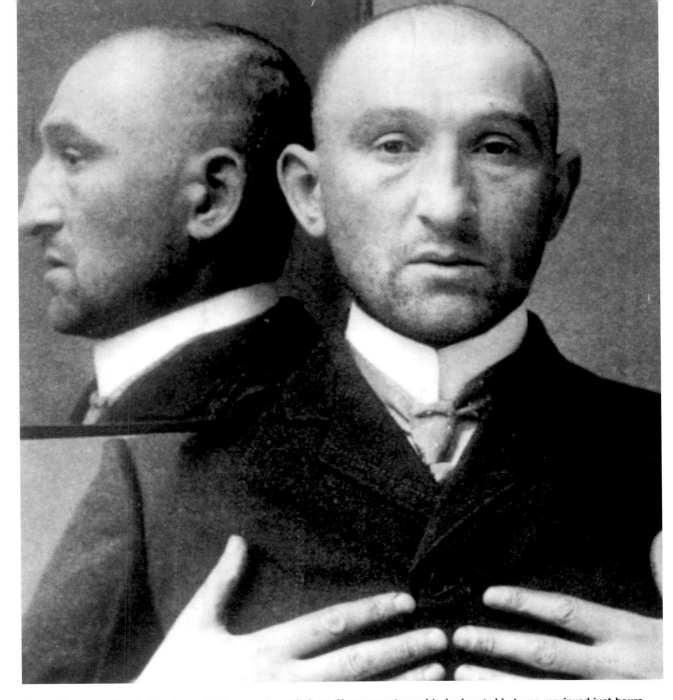

Oscar Slater was the victim of an outrageous police stitch-up. He was sentenced to be hanged but was reprieved just hours before he was due to die and spent almost nineteen years in prison. As in the case of Paddy Meehan many years later, a flawed identity parade was involved. In reality, there was barely a stitch of evidence against him. He had an alibi and he returned from America voluntarily to face trial, so sure was he that no one could convict him. But he went down just the same. This is a 1909 Peterhead shot.

In the Slater case, it is now obvious that the police had an agenda and were hell bent on convicting him regardless of the facts. One brave detective, Lieutenant John Trench, broke ranks some years after Slater was framed to go public on how the case was wrongly handled. He was rewarded by being dismissed from the police. He died in 1919 but, many years later, an inquiry found that Trench had acted with 'moral conviction' and in 1999 a commemorative panel dedicated to his memory went on display in force HQ in Pitt Street.

The wrongful conviction of Slater was so outrageous that, again like Meehan, it attracted the attention of the top writers of the day. The creator of Sherlock Holmes, Sir Arthur Conan Doyle was among those to take up the case. And the author of fiction's most famous detective stories was much used to drawing conclusions from evidence.

As for Slater, a German Jew who had come to Scotland, he seems to have been remarkably generous in spirit to the country that treated him so badly and he stayed on to enjoy a pleasant retirement in Ayr. Here he is with his bowler with jaunty air. He made many friends and lived out the rest of his life in genteel respectability.

Compliments of Oscar Slater.

This has to be one of the most remarkable images in the *Herald/Times* archive. Photographers were seldom around in the thirties when the big gang fights, often involving hundreds, took place. The sheer size of some of the battles is a surprise to many of today's commentators. This is Tollcross Road in 1933 with women and children, as well as decent hard-working men in collars and ties, fleeing in terror as gangsters settle some bloody dispute.

CHAPTER THREE

Blood, Bread and Beer

Glasgow was no stranger to violence even in the eighteenth and nineteenth centuries. In fact, the pitched battles between rival gangs on Glasgow Green in the late twenties and thirties were much smaller that those of the Bread Riot of 1848, said to be the largest example of mass violence in the city's history. More than 3,000 people went on a rampage on this infamous occasion. The Glasgow Green meeting had originally been arranged by the Chartists, a movement committed to fighting social injustice. There may have been fine words spoken on the Green but it all ended up with street fighting of a bloody nature with iron railings in Monteith Row being torn up and the mob marching on the city centre. Shops and businesses were looted and even a gun shop raided and the stolen weapons fired into the air in douce Buchanan Street.

Several people died before the rioters were driven back into the east end (in future years this would be the prime locus for much of the violence in the city). Early attempts to control the menacing mob by the forerunners of the police force and members of the city guard failed and the rioting went on for more than twenty-four hours before the army managed to disperse the crowds. Some of the rioters were transported to Australia for their part in the fight for 'social justice'.

But this was not the first occasion when the streets of this remarkable old city were home to violent crowds. Nor would it be the last! Long before the Chartists were formed, the city had suffered during the Beer Riots. In 1772 the government made a bad mistake and courted trouble when a swingeing increase in tax on a barrel of beer was levied. Messing around with the price of the working man's pint is never good politics and this did not go down well with the lieges. In addition, the Jacobites were said at the time to be in a state of 'thinly veiled rebellion'. Sizeable riots ensued and it required six troops of Dragoon and Highlanders to restore order.

But it took until around the turn of the twentieth century for what we would now recognise as organised gangs to emerge from the slums and deprivation of a rough, tough seaport

The fearsome threat posed by a broken bottle – the weapon so beloved of the early gangs – is obvious here. The police will tell you that one of its attractions was that it was easy to hide about your person and, before it was smashed, there was always an excuse for carrying it – the innocent desire to slake your thirst. But the bottle of beer that was transformed in an instant into a weapon could do horrific damage to an opponent. The injuries it created tested the skill of the city's experienced casualty surgeons to the full.

According to the archive, this is Bridgeton Cross in the fifties but I suspect this photograph was taken much earlier. There are plenty of cloth caps and hard faces as Bridgeton residents take their ease. It was around the famous 'umbrella' that, in the thirties, the Billy Boys' band used to bring drill nights to a close with a rousing rendition of 'God Save the King'.

city. Many citizens were honest toilers in the docks, shipyards, coalfields and various forms of heavy industry, who were content to earn their corn with sweat on their brows in the hellholes that provided employment for those who wanted it. Then, as now, others were averse to hard work and, tempted by the shortcuts to wealth offered by a life of crime, went in for extortion, burglary and violence.

The earliest records of what could be called gangs note the activities of the Penny Mob, which seems to have been formed in the late 1880s. In the years to follow, literally hundreds of gangs were to blight the city but the Penny Mob have the distinction – if it can be called that – of being the first to capture the public imagination. Their name came from the fact that their members paid in a penny a week to a sort of benevolent fund, the cash to be used to pay fines and feed womenfolk and children when members ended up behind bars. But this was no benign Robin Hood sort of outfit – the newspapers of the time make it clear that they were a dangerous band of hooligans. Yellowing cuttings tell of battles between the Penny Mob and other gangs, such as the Wee Do'e Hill and the Big Do'e Hill. This was before the time of the razor as the pre-eminent weapon and these battles were largely fought with broken whinstone (there was plenty around as railways were being built in many parts of the city), paling stobs, washing boiler lids, thick leather belts and sometimes just fists. The Penny Mob survived in various forms till the late thirties and were still around when Percy Sillitoe arrived as first official and successful 'gangbuster'.

The two main gangs in pre-Second World War era were, of course, the Bridgeton Billy Boys and their sectarian enemies, the Norman Conks. The Billy Boys were led by the infamous 'King Billy' Fullerton and the Conks by 'Bull' Bowman. But there were many other major gangs, now largely forgotten. The Redskins were big news around 1916. The reports of the day may be rather circumspect by modern standards but it is not hard to get their drift when they talk of thirty or forty youths rampaging around the streets near Bridgeton Cross sweeping all in their paths aside and shouting, 'We are the ★★★★★★★ Redskins!' During the First World War, this gang alone was said to have around 1,000 members, a couple of hundred more than even the much better remembered Billy Boys could claim. On one infamous occasion the Redskins even hijacked a tramcar!

Much of this violence was taking place around the time of the heyday of the early Hollywood westerns and it is easy to see where the name Redskins came from – even if the American prairies were several thousand miles from Parkhead. The Goucho and the Gringo are others with a nod in the direction of the Wild West. But many of the other gang names are of more mysterious origins – like the Bloodhound Flying Squad or the Ging Gong. Show business always seems to have had an influence and, in more modern times, you had the UNCLE in Ruchill and THRUSH in Townhead, presumably taken from the David McCallum TV series *The Man from UNCLE*.

Other older gangs of the thirties were the Beehive and the Parlour Boys who were based in the south side's Bedford Parlour Dance Hall in Celtic Street. This group was led by a thug called

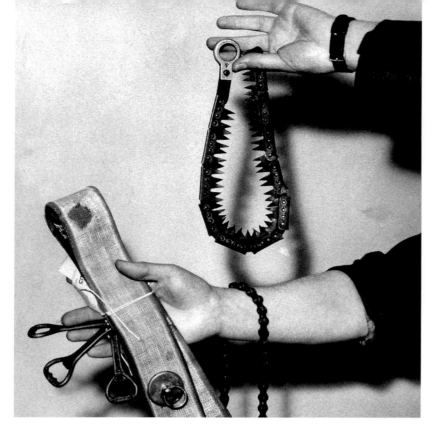

These were photographed at the Central Police Court in July 1952. The chain has sharpened points to increase its efficiency in slashing through skin, muscle and bone. Likewise, the belt has been weighted with bottle openers and sink plugs to assist in causing maximum damage when swung in battle. The armoury of the gang thug was inventive. Sometimes improvised bolas-style weapons were created out of cord and heavy nuts and bolts. And open razors, axes, carpet knives and machetes and swords could also be pressed into use.

James Dalziel who died after an affray in the hall. The change in social mores over the years is demonstrated by the fact that Dalziel, nicknamed 'Razzle Dazzle', when in the hall, only danced with male members of his gang – to tread the light fantastic with a girl was considered a sign of weakness!

There is no doubt, however, that the most infamous of the gangs was the Billy Boys. They were led by Billy Fullerton, an interesting character who steered clear of thieving and other conventional crimes but enjoyed pitting his men against the Norman Conks. Weapons of choice for both sides in these bloody battles were pick shafts measuring forty-two inches in length, hatchets, sharpened bicycle chains, razors and broken bottles. The Billy Boys were a highly disciplined group and, in the manner of the Belfast gangs, had

their own band. After drill nights, they would march to Bridgeton Cross and play 'God Save the King' before dispersing. Even the man who was largely responsible for their demise, Sir Percy Sillitoe, paid tribute to the generalship of their leader Fullerton.

Sillitoe's reputation now is mainly that of a gangbuster and, to this end, as noted, he met force with force. On arrival as head of the city's force, he set about assembling an elite squad nicknamed the 'Untouchables' – these were the biggest, bravest men in the force who were as good with their fists as the gangs themselves. This was long before the era of political correctness and, on many occasions, when trouble was brewing on the dark streets, the Untouchables would retaliate first, as they say, and plunge into the mobs, fists and batons flying. He also used the mounted branch – nicknamed

If the weapons of the gangs could instil fear into their opponents, Sir Percy Sillitoe (right), an imposing figure in uniform, had the same effect on the bad guys themselves. 'The Big Fella' was getting the thirties gangs under control when the Second World War intervened. Sillitoe formed an elite squad of handpicked tough cops to tackle the thugs, meeting violence with violence. He used informers to enable his men to ambush gangs and built up the mounted branch, known as Sillitoe's Cossacks, into an impressive fighting force that was adept at breaking up inflammatory parades and random gang battles.

Sillitoe's Cossacks – to great effect to break up marches and demonstrations. And there was plenty of work here – the Billy Boys liked nothing better than marching provocatively through streets they knew to be largely Catholic, the flute band blowing their lungs out and the big drum thumping out a message of menace. And, in turn, the Conks and their supporters in such streets liked nothing better than leaning out top-floor windows and throwing everything from boiling water to excrement on to the heads of the marchers. It was, as Sillitoe observed, often like some medieval siege.

Sir Percy may have been a man who condoned violence from the boys in blue when it was, in his view, required but he was far from an unthinking cop. He was ahead of his time in the use of informers to find out where the gang fights were

due to take place and quick to ambush the would-be mobs and defuse the trouble. He also pioneered the radio cars (Glasgow was the original choice for the filming of TV's Z-Cars) so beloved of the modern cops and he was he first to have an underwater squad to search for weapons ditched into murky waters.

To his men, Percy Sillitoe was a legend – his men referred to him as 'The Big Fella' or 'The Captain'. There are some today who think that his robust approach is just what is needed to curb the excesses of the current crop of neds and no-goods who still make headlines. Be that as it may, there is a daily reminder of the great gangbuster on the streets of the city. It was Sillitoe who introduced the black and white check ribbons on the coppers' hats – a style since adopted by many police forces round the world.

Not all the folk sentenced by fate to live in the slums succumbed to a life of crime. Many made the most of it, creating little palaces with gleaming ranges, the centrepiece of tenement life. One good armchair was a real luxury. This evocative shot of Annie Knox enjoying the warmth of the fire while her son Ernest naps was taken in a room and kitchen in The Dwellings, Green Street, Bridgeton, in the thirties.

This picture shows how the squalor and neglected living conditions lingered on in the Gorbals, Bridgeton, much of the east end and areas like Garscube Road and Maryhill, on the west side of the city, until as late as the sixties. Such archive images demonstrate just how hard it must have been to bring up families on the straight and narrow – though most did manage to do so. Such deprivation, combined with unemployment, illnesses and a general sense of hopelessness, acted as recruiting sergeants for gangs which offered some degree of comradeship and the excitement of street battles. There was also the bonus of cash from extortion, burglary and crimes that were often perpetrated on the poor folk who were the gangsters' neighbours.

Face-to-face battles often took place to establish leadership of a gang. The toughest would be recognised as the boss and challenges had to be faced down – violently. The infamous 'Glasgow Kiss' – a head butt into the face of an opponent – was often a feature of such fights. Street fighting is always a dirty business as this photograph shows. Even if no weapons were involved, a good kicking or kneeing in the face were deemed fair tactics. The Queensberry rules had no input into such disputes.

Few photographs exist of the infamous gang leaders of the thirties. This ordinary-looking man in a bunnet was an extraordinary figure in the criminal history of the city. He is 'King Billy' Fullerton and, in his pomp, he commanded a mini-army of Billy Boys and took part in some legendary battles with his sectarian enemies the Norman Conks and Chief Constable Percy Sillitoe's 'Untouchables' and 'Cossacks'. Sillitoe is on record as admiring Fullerton's abilities as a leader though he fought him and his thugs mercilessly. Fullerton died in 1962 aged seventy-five and was given a real gangland send-off, with around a thousand gathering to watch the funeral party leave a Bridgeton tenement for Riddrie Park cemetery. In a symbolic touch, the cortege stopped the traffic at Bridgeton Cross and, for part of the way to the cemetery, a flute band led the procession.

Pub culture played a big role in crime in times past, particularly in areas with bad housing. The bar was a welcome escape and drouthy folk, tired out after a day in the yards or steel works, mingled with others with less acceptable ploys in mind – many a break-in or gang battle would be planned in the boozers of the city. This shot gives some idea of the atmosphere in the pubs of the sixties. Writer Jack House seems in pensive mood in Cloughley's Bar near the old Maryhill Tram depot. It's all a long way from the gastro pubs and wine bars of today.

CHAPTER FOUR

Black Outs, Bricks and Bank Robbery

For many elderly Glaswegians, the abiding memory of the Second World War is of blackouts, food rationing, clothing coupons and a life of austerity played out against the scary background music of air-raid sirens, usually followed by the sound of Nazi bombers droning overhead – dark days indeed. But, for one breed of Glaswegian, this was the time of opportunity. Walter Norval was the leader of a lawless gang of thugs who staged a series of spectacular bank robberies. He went on to become the city's first Godfather but, during the war, he was a youngster and he remembers the blackouts as being the perfect time for him to begin a career in crime. No street lighting and houses with the windows covered in heavy blackout cloth made the shop windows of wartime streets tempting targets for a brick or two. Walter and his ilk had a carefully refined technique. They used to wait until a tram was rumbling past the target – to drown the noise of breaking glass – and then smash their way into the shop, via the broken window, and make off with whatever happened to be available. Rolls of cloth for suits,

eggs, ham, drink – it all ended up in the black market that flourished at the time.

With his father dead and his mother busy with other matters, Norval was left to fend for himself. Norval was not unique in this – many other kids were in the same position. During both world wars of the twentieth century, there was an upsurge in crime, particularly among youngsters. Fathers were away in the services and mothers were working in munitions factories or whatever. Even the police force was depleted and the sort of good men who, in peacetime, would be running youth clubs, BB battalions and Scout troops were away in uniform. In the Second World War, rationing also played a role in the increase in crime by creating a black market where stolen goods of all kinds could be turned into readies without the slightest trouble. This was a time before TV and home entertainment and the working man, spared from enlistment to the services because he was in a job of national importance in a shipyard, steelworks or mine, spent as much time as he could afford in the pub where the landlord or the barman would be delighted to

This is Patrick Carracher who ended his days being dragged screaming to the gallows in the Bar-L in 1945. A classic case of the lone-wolf razor-slasher, he didn't run with the gangs but created enough mayhem on his own. He murdered John Gordon from Aitken Street.

get half a dozen prized eggs, a chicken or some ham or butter to pass on at a profit to his customers. Stolen clothing coupons or booze and cigarettes were also in demand.

It got worse when the war was over. Many men returned to their home patch unsettled and unable to find work. Many, too, brought home revolvers or other weapons either stolen from the British Army or plundered during the Allies' march across Europe. Gun crime took a dramatic rise immediately post-war. But the lawlessness that was around also caused an increase in that old Glasgow curse – razor-slashing. One man who stamped his presence on the years after the Hitler war ended was Lord John Carmont. This judge, a kindly, quiet man away from the courts, believed that the only way to stop the slashings that were becoming commonplace was by the imposition of long sentences – so much so that, to this day, criminals given a particularly tough sentence are said to be 'doing a Carmont'. His policy did little to affect the long-term trends but, for a few years, his belief in locking the offenders up and metaphorically throwing away the key worked. The *Glasgow Herald* editorialised, saying:

> His salutary sentences on razor-slashers, and knife-wielders, in Glasgow High Court in the years following the Second World War had a marked effect on the criminal classes and earned him the respect and approval of law-abiding citizens.

The noble lord's sentences certainly made the criminals think about what they were up to. Walter Norval told me that, at the time, the city's huge army of dangerous men were well aware that Carmont was a practising Catholic and, in this city so filled with

Tony Miller: became almost resigned to the sentence of death and put all his faith in God's will.

Another man to die in the Bar-L hanging shed was ex-policeman James Robertson in 1950. A very different set of circumstances from Carracher's led to his death – indeed, if he wished, it seemed he could have escaped the noose. He killed his mistress by running his car back and forward over her body in Prospecthill Road in the south side. The legendary Laurence Dowdall defended him and said later of the case, 'His wife knew he had been conducting this liaison but he said he was not going to let her down in public. If he had told the truth about her, he would have got off. The very first question the prosecution asked was "What was Miss McCluskey [the mistress] to you?"' Robertson answered this with 'A casual acquaintance.' and, in doing so, he turned a crime of passion into a senseless killing.

Tony Miller became the last person to be hanged in Barlinnie when he died, aged just nineteen, in 1960. Again, looking back, it seems he should not have been executed and his case did much to fire the public revulsion that led to the end of the death penalty. He had been convicted of killing a homosexual in Queen's Park after an accomplice, who was also charged, claimed that Miller had struck the fatal blow in a joint attack. The case attracted huge public attention and 30,000 signed a petition to spare him. And, in a 1995 book, the redoubtable city lawyer Len Murray recalled that, significantly, one of the grounds of an appeal made by Miller was that the judge, Lord Wheatley, failed to offer the jury the option of culpable homicide which did not carry the death penalty. But the law took its course and Miller died a few days before Christmas.

Some call Glasgow the Chicago of north-west Europe and, like that city on the shores of Lake Michigan, we had our own 'Scarface' – but here we see not Alphonse Capone but Victor Russo, a Lanarkshire villain who made all sorts of headlines. This shot of Russo, taken in 1950, shows him looking for all the world like a mob foot soldier from a Hollywood gangster movie. Never in the really top league of crime, he nonetheless caused the police much bother down the years and is well remembered by the old criminal hands still alive.

sectarian hatred, there was much speculation over pints in the seedier pubs about how the judge's religion would affect his sentencing. This, curiously, was unlucky for Willie Collins, the first 'Catholic' slasher to appear before him. The judge had just sentenced two men, who had so massively cut up the faces of their opponents that they needed dozens of stitches, to five and seven years respectively. Collins' offence was hardly in the same class – his victim required only two stitches. He got ten years – five years a stitch, as the underworld noted. The point was made and no one could ever claim Lord Carmont was a soft touch.

But by the time the forties had run their course, crime in the city was taking on a new face. A different type of gang culture was emerging – the new crooks were just as ruthless and violent as the old criminal tribes had been but they favoured a different approach. Thugs still roamed the streets slashing and putting the boot in on rivals who dared to invade their turf. They still broke into homes, terrorised publicans and their customers and indulged in bloody assault for a few quid or none. But the evil seeds of the modern drug wars and the gangs who fight to control them were beginning to be sown.

The classic example is the XYY gang controlled by that tough old nut Walter Norval. Until he came along, gangs were often based in one area in particular, seldom venturing outside their territory. Norval had his own patch – indeed he was known as 'The King of the Twilight Zone', a seedy area between Garscube Road and the city centre proper – but, when he turned to bank robbery (he wasn't involved in the drugs scene that dominated the ethos of the gangs and Godfathers who were to succeed him), he cast his net wider. He realised that a carefully put together collection of villains, no matter where they came from in the city, would be more powerful than any gang of local thugs.

A career criminal even from his immediately post-teens days, he was a shrewd organiser and planner and banks and payrolls had a fascination for him. And, before he was sent to Peterhead for a stretch lasting many years – he blames his downfall on a treacherous gang member – he had a long run of highly profitable armed robberies that, for a spell, baffled the cops. At his peak, he had an army of informers to point his boys in the direction of an easy cash touch. He worked at it – gang members disguised as workmen studied payroll runs and getaway routes and they rehearsed carefully for their big hits. It was a different world from the old gangs – though one similarity was that the man at the top was the toughest of the tough. Norval ruled his foot soldiers with his fists and his guns. They did what they were told.

Not all the violence was down to gangs. Glasgow had more than its fair share of what the cops like to call domestics – disputes between husbands and wives or lovers (or bidie-ins in the local parlance). Poverty, lack of work, too much drink or drugs strain relationships to violent breaking point. In the outlying schemes and city centre slums, there were many murders that in France would be classed as 'crimes of passion'. It is a phrase a tad too elegant to cover the sight of a body lying in the street, covered with a blanket, blood flowing out from under it on to the pavement – something a detective on the beat would become familiar with.

Walter Norval is generally accepted to be the first of the modern era of Glasgow Godfathers. A wily lawbreaker, he saw the advantages, back in the seventies, of several criminal factions linking up under his leadership. Bank and payroll robberies were his speciality and he ended up doing a long stretch in Peterhead.

Here is Norval in his prime in 1977 enjoying the fruits of criminality on a balcony in the Spanish sun. The sweet life was soon to end and porridge and cocoa took the place of paella and vodka.

Prison never broke Norval's spirit. He survived long years behind bars, staying fit in the gym and keeping a finger on what was going on around town in Glasgow. He finally left his last prison, Penninghame, near Newton Stewart, to much comment from the prison officers of the 'Who says crime doesn't pay?' variety. He drove from the jail with his connections in a gold Rolls Royce. Here he stops to pose roadside for a snap with his daughter Rita.

As a kid on the streets around Garscube Road, Norval and his first gang, the Wee Mob, hung out with such infamous local villains as John Foy of Caithness Street and Joe O'Hara of Lyon Street. They took a shine to Walter, seeing him as a cocky, fearless youth who was obviously destined to cause much trouble. One haunt was the Tower Ballroom building at the Round Toll. These days the 'tower' is much emasculated and the snooker hall where Norval and Co. spent the traditional wasted youth is no more.

Norval's final demise as a big-time gangster fascinated the papers. The man they called 'The King of the Twilight Zone' went out with a smile as this shot of him and his lieutenants leaving court in 1977 after sentencing shows. The High Court was firebombed just before his trial but it went ahead – and lasted sixteen days – before it ended with sentences totalling seventy-four years being handed down. Scotland's first major crime syndicate was broken. Norval got fourteen years, John 'Plum' McDuff, a henchman he had recruited during a previous spell in Peterhead, got twenty-one years and Joseph Polding, aka 'The Mallet', got eighteen years. Other gang members got shorter sentences.

The lock 'em up and throw away the key approach was only one weapon on the war on crime. There was growing concern in the late sixties about the activities of young, lawless gangs making life hell on the streets of the post-war schemes. The idea of the Easterhouse Project was to give idle hands something worthwhile to do and, thereby, defuse the tensions. Liverpudlian song-and-dance man Frankie Vaughan, seen here with some Easterhouse kids, got involved while he was appearing as a headliner at the old Alhambra. A long-time hard worker with the Association of Boys' Clubs, he threw his weight behind the Project.

Lord Carmont presided over a decline in slashings and knife attacks in the fifties. He adopted a policy of long sentences and the word soon got around the thugs that he was no pushover and to appear before him was bad news indeed – so much so that criminals still refer to a long sentence as 'doing a Carmont'. But, as with many other clampdowns on the gangs before and after Carmont, the effect on the crime statistics was temporary.

A feature of the Project was a weapons amnesty. Here local youngsters gawp at weapons dumped in bins left on waste ground for that purpose.

The Easterhouse weapons amnesty wasn't the only one in the sixties. Here is a frightening haul from a citywide gun amnesty – striking proof of the number of firearms in circulation.

This shot taken inside the Easterhouse Project premises right at the start shows Jack House chatting with John Samson, the Project's assistant director. The table tennis equipment is there – and so is the graffiti. Chief Constable James Robertson was supportive of the Project, as were many local sports stars. There was a hard core of local workers to push it forward and the verdict of history is that it did much good.

Murders involving children were also not uncommon and one legendary city detective told me that, after visiting a crime scene where children lay dead on the floor of a flat, surrounded by blood-splattered walls, he couldn't face food for a week. And he never ever could forget the scene in that house in Govan – not even almost sixty years later.

Crime had another unchanging face. The world of the teenage thug was, dispiritingly, as bad in the post-war sink schemes as it had been in the Bridgeton and Gorbals slums of the thirties. A new council house with inside toilet was no guarantee

that the younger inhabitants would keep out of trouble. It didn't help that the giant schemes constructed by the old Glasgow Corporation – with good intentions but little foresight – were bereft of cinemas, youth clubs, swimming pools or libraries or any of the other diversions that could have kept youngsters occupied. One Glasgow comedian famously called such areas 'deserts wi windaes'.

It was particularly bad in the late sixties in Easterhouse and the efforts of the locals to do something about it caught the attention of the famous entertainer Frankie Vaughan, then

Although he was criticised by small-minded right-wing councillors, there is no doubt that the glamour of Frankie Vaughan's involvement helped the project. And if you are a big recording artist and variety star, you wear your sharpest gear at all times – even at the risk of a splashing or two.

appearing at the old Alhambra, and he decided to do his bit to help. The Easterhouse Project was headline stuff from day one. The song-and-dance man was criticised for talking to the gang leaders but he persisted. There was a weapons amnesty that brought press people from all over Europe to witness young gangsters dumping weapons of all sorts into heaps to be collected by the police.

Plans were made for a clubhouse in the area and the army offered to help build it. For a spell, the papers were full of little else – and that included the criticisms of local right-wing politicians who thought there was too much pandering to the

gangs. 'Jail them, don't build them clubhouses,' was their motto. But big names from stage and sport and folk who simply wanted to do something positive about the problem pushed on with the Project and the police gave their support. It is interesting to note that, when, many years later, the crime figures for the time were published, they showed that there had been a measurable fall in gangsterism and street violence. Sadly Frankie Vaughan didn't live to see this official vindication – he died before the figures were published. But he lives on in the memory of the people of Easter-house, now a much-improved place to live in.

A familiar sight on the city streets was the police bus used to transport prisoners from jail to court and vice versa. The menacing black vehicle with its unseen cargo of lowlifes was a normal part of the morning and evening rush hours.

Taking delivery of a new car is a day to remember and here traffic officers admire the line-up of highly polished patrol cars ready for action on the streets.

As many of the photographs in this book show, detectives spend much time trudging the rain-soaked streets with collar turned up and soft hat firmly fixed on the head but, back in the office, 'thinking time' is a must. Here Tom Goodall, one of the most famous detectives to serve in the city force, ponders his next move in a murder investigation.

This is a familiar face of evil – the mug shot of Peter Manuel was much used in the media at the time of his trial and it is not forgotten by the citizens of this city and many areas around it.

CHAPTER FIVE

The Man Who Ran to the Gallows

It is always interesting to examine the difference between fame and infamy. Glasgow has traditionally been famous worldwide for the friendliness of its inhabitants, its top-class heavy industries like locomotive and shipbuilding and its lively theatres and dance halls. It is, without dispute, infamous, in the real sense of the word, for its history of gangs and violence. Some of that infamy springs also from sensational miscarriages of justice like the Oscar Slater case and the imprisonment of Patrick Connolly Meehan and the unsolved mystery of the Bible John murders. But Glasgow also has a 'world-class' entrant in the league table of infamous serial killers – Peter Manuel.

Manuel may not have been a true resident of the city but he died in it – in the Barlinnie hanging shed, at 8 a.m. on Friday, 11 July 1958. In a short life of violent evil – he was thirty-two when he faced the hangman – he preyed on its citizens, and those of nearby areas, spreading a fear that is hard for anyone who did not live through the Manuel era to comprehend. There were few households

who did not hold their breath over breakfast that morning as the clock hands moved slowly to the appointed hour for the killer to step into eternity. It is said, incidentally, that, in the end, with the macabre game finally up, he ran the last few steps to the rope.

That he should be executed had a touch of irony in it. Before his final sensational trial in the old High Court in Glasgow, he had had many brushes with the law and had been incarcerated in Peterhead, among other places, and, when there, he liked to boast to fellow inmates that his father had died in the electric chair in America. It was a fantasy, like much of the thinking of this evil man. There was, however, a connection with the States. Manuel had been born in Manhattan when his parents had temporarily moved across the Atlantic to seek work for a few years, before returning to the UK and settling for a spell in Coventry and then moving north to Lanarkshire.

The final act in the Manuel story was sensational. Each day, hundreds watched as the accused and the lawyers arrived in court for a trial

In January 1956, the news of the discovery of the body of a pretty seventeen-year-old called Anne Kneillands on an East Kilbride golf course shocked newspaper readers. It sparked a grim manhunt that was made all the more difficult by bitter weather as this scene near the discovery point shows.

Anne Kneillands, seen here in a party dress, was one of three attractive teenagers killed by the monster that was Peter Manuel. Despite his confession, he was acquitted at his trial on this particular murder charge as there was no independent corroboration.

Police hunt for clues in the Kneillands case in frost-hardened ground near the fifth tee of an East Kilbride golf course.

that attracted worldwide attention and was covered by dozens of newspapers and TV and radio stations. It is not too often that the man in the dock is accused of eight deaths and suspected, if uncharged, of the killings of others. Manuel was accused of killing, in separate incidents, two attractive young seventeen-year-olds, Anne Kneillands and Isabelle Cooke. In addition, he was accused of killing master baker William Watt's wife, Marion, their sixteen-year-old daughter, Vivienne, and Mrs Margaret Brown of Glasgow, William Watt's sister-in law. And he was alleged to have also murdered Peter and Doris Smart and their ten-year-old son Michael.

Much was made at the time of his decision during the course of the trial to dismiss the top men in his defence team and take on the role of trying to dodge the noose himself. But in retrospect there was little prospect of that ever happening. He had confessed to killing Anne Kneillands, whose body was found on an East Kilbride golf course. But there was no corroborating evidence to this claim so, under Scots Law, the judge directed that he should be acquitted on this charge. He had also admitted the killing of Isabelle Cooke under questioning and this time there was corroboration – he had indicated where the body could be found! And his claim of alibi in the case of the Smarts foundered. There was also enough to convict in the case of the break-in at the Watts' bungalow. But this incident provided a sensational diversion.

Before the High Court trial William Watt himself was wrongly accused of killing his own family and spent sixty-seven days in Barlinnie. On the night of the murder, he had been on fishing

Metal detectors are used to sweep the Fennsbank garden and nearby areas in search of the weapon that killed the Watts and Mrs Brown.

There was no fancy digital or video equipment in those days but pictures of every scene of possible interest were snapped by the police photographers.

trip to Cairnbaan, west of Lochgilphead. Witnesses saw him at breakfast at 8 a.m. The victims had been shot at around 6 a.m. and some cops believed bizarrely that Watt had travelled to Glasgow, committed the crime and returned to Argyll to establish an alibi. It was a nonsense. Even today, it is a hard two-hour journey each way, even for someone with Schumacher tendencies. But the case against Watt was further flawed. He was picked out of an identify parade after his photograph had appeared in a newspaper. And

claims that he had been seen on the Renfrew ferry and driving around Loch Lomondside were also confused and suspect. A further clincher in his favour was that, at breakfast time in Argyll, the car in which he was supposed to have made this remarkable journey was still cold and frost covered! It was yet another example of the pressure of public opinion on the police to get a 'result' in a shocking murder case causing the finger of guilt to be pointed in totally the wrong direction. Shades of Meehan and Slater!

Vivienne Watt has her mother Marion's hands on her shoulders in this group posing for a snap for the family album.

A long ordeal is about to begin for the man the papers liked to call the 'master baker' as William Watt, wrongly suspected of being involved in the killing of his family, drives away from Rutherglen police office during inquiries.

Another for the album – this time William Watt, who was initially accused of the murders, has his arm round his wife Marion's shoulders.

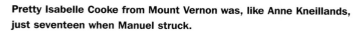

Pretty Isabelle Cooke from Mount Vernon was, like Anne Kneillands, just seventeen when Manuel struck.

This is the shallow grave, near her home, in which Isabelle Cooke's body was concealed. Manuel had eventually directed the police to where it could be found.

As in the earlier murders, the police knew that they were hunting a fiend who could strike again at any moment so there was real urgency in their search for clues in the fields, burns and ponds near the place where Isabelle's body was found.

The Watt business produced some of the highest drama at the trial. Giving evidence against the man who killed his family, the baker had to attend court either on crutches or wheeled in on a stretcher, having suffered an accident before the trial. Manuel, in his last role as an interrogative lawyer, insisted in cross-examining Watt and claimed in court that the master baker was the killer. The face-to-face encounter between them was unforgettable. In a final address, Manuel spoke to the jury for three hours and, although he was later praised for his skill by Lord Cameron, some of what he said was decidedly lame, including the remark, 'I can only say I have not murdered any of these people. I have no reason to murder these people.' As I noted in a previous book on the case it was not quite in the Perry Mason or Laurence Dowdall class of pleading.

Manuel, who after conviction confessed to other killings, was clearly destined to make the walk from the condemned cell to the gallows. He did so despite a late attempt to fake mental illness. But, when the trap dropped at precisely 8 a.m. that fateful morning, Glasgow collectively sighed 'good riddance' and got back to normal life after a period when the evil doings of an uncaught serial killer had spread fear into every corner of the city.

During the investigations into the Manuel killings, the underwater squad had a particularly harrowing task searching dangerous, muddy ponds.

Isabelle Cooke's father and her brother lead the mourners in a bleak, windswept Riddrie cemetery in January 1958.

No stone will be left unturned is a cliché but it is often almost literally true. As in the Watt case, metal detectors were used near the Cooke home.

Peter and Doris Smart were in their forties and their son Michael was ten years old when they were killed during a break-in at their Uddingston home by Manuel. Peter Smart was the manager of an engineering firm. Defending himself in court, Manuel claimed that he had an alibi for this triple killing – he didn't.

Rowing boats on the Clyde were commandeered in the search for the gun that killed the Smarts.

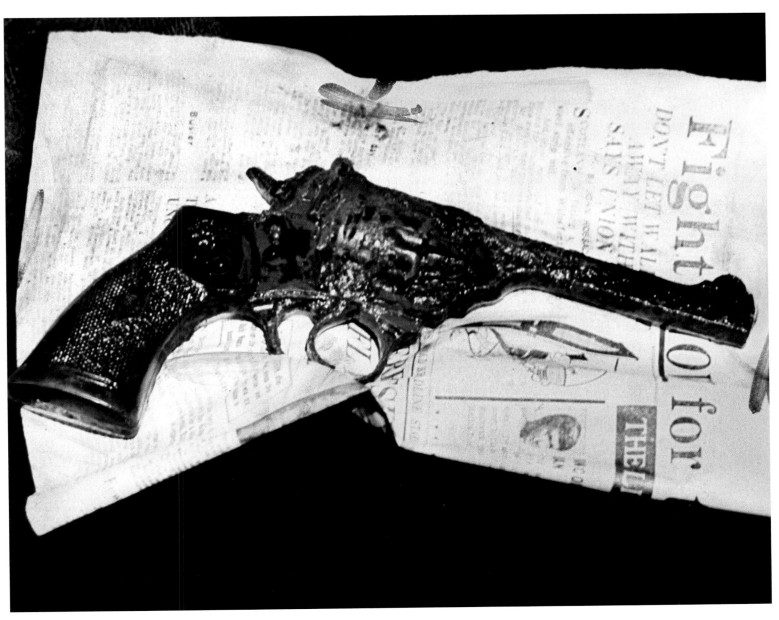

Divers in old-fashioned helmets finally located the Webley revolver used by Manuel in the Fennsbank massacre. It was a vital clue that meant the noose was looming.

The news that there was a suspect in the series of killings that had shocked Glasgow and its surrounds brought out the crowds. Here Manuel is driven back to prison after an appearance at Hamilton, at this stage charged with only four murders. He was charged with eight killings in the High Court and convicted of seven but it is thought he was responsible for several more.

The hottest ticket in town – this is just part of the first-day queue for the public galleries when Manuel finally appeared in the dock.

A pre-trial accident meant that William Watt arrived at court on a stretcher or sometimes on crutches. A wheelchair was made available for him during his ordeal in court, where he met the man who had slaughtered his family face to face.

When William Watt was arrested, it was ludicrously postulated that he had driven through the night from Cairnbaan to murder his own family and then returned in the dark to breakfast in his hotel. He is seen here in his big Vauxhall. Keen driver as he was, what had been suggested was impossible given the time frame of the murders and he was released from Barlinnie as there really was no evidence against him. He later gave his own evidence and this helped to send the real killer to the gallows.

Watt was enjoying a fishing holiday in beautiful Cairnbaan, Argyll, on the banks of the Crinan Canal, the night his family was killed.

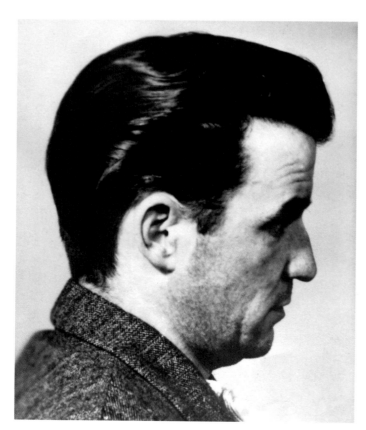

Mass murderer Peter
Manuel in profile.

High Street is filled with frenzied crowds waiting for the final verdict in the Manuel trial, which had dominated the news for sixteen days.

The entrance to Glasgow Green, overlooked by the grim grandeur of the High Court and ironically not far from the scene of historic public executions like that of Dr Pritchard, was also filled with a throng eager to hear that the man who had terrorised the city for years was to pay the final price on the scaffold.

A shackled Manuel is taken into the High Court in Edinburgh by the back door for the inevitable appeal against the death sentence. It failed.

This mug shot of Arthur Thompson Sr gives some idea of the menace of the true hard man.

270591 DA052405

CHAPTER SIX

Bullets and Battles at the Ponderosa

Glaswegians have always enjoyed what they like to call 'a night at the pictures', with westerns and gangster epics particular specialities. Walter Norval, the city's first Godfather, liked nothing better than watching the exploits of Dillinger and the other big-time mobsters celebrated by Hollywood. Indeed, in his pomp and dressed in the good suit for visiting a nightclub or casino, he would have given George Raft a run for his money. Norval admits to picking up a few wrinkles on bank robbing from his hours spent in the city's fleapits. And there's no doubt that the old-time gang the Redskins, now largely forgotten but once a fearsome outfit, appropriated the name from the westerns that were so popular even before the days of the talkies. Interestingly it is said that 'Tongs ya bass', that most infamous of Glasgow gang slogans, was also inspired by Hollywood, in particular one movie featuring the blood-letting of the Chinese tongs in gory detail. It so stimulated young neds in the audience that they are said to have left the cinema shouting, 'Tongs ya bass!' and hurling bricks through windows and other such violent diversions. A legendary slogan was born!

The influence of the western on Glasgow gangland stretched into the TV age. The Ponderosa of the vastly popular series *Bonanza* was a somewhat idyllic western ranch, a place of rolling plains, where cow punching was mixed with a dash of gun-slinging and territorial disputes. Glasgow borrowed the name for its own Ponderosa, a much-extended house near Hogganfield Loch in the eastern approaches to the city. The name may have been nicked, appropriately, from a TV western but this was a place known and feared by all in the underworld. Cows were the least likely things to be punched around these parts. But disputes over the control of territory were commonplace. A heavily protected fortress, the Ponderosa was the home of the man they call 'The Last Godfather' – Arthur Thompson Sr whose life story is brilliantly told in Reg McKay's bestseller of that name.

Thompson and his predecessor as Godfather, Norval, did a little 'business' together from time to time but the removal of Walter to do a long stretch

The house on the far right is Thompson's home – the infamous Ponderosa, named after a ranch in the popular TV series *Bonanza*. From here he mercilessly ruled much of the city's criminal elite for many blood-soaked years.

in Peterhead left Glasgow wide open for Thompson and his lieutenants. They grabbed the chance and for years they terrorised areas of the city, with extortion and moneylending their particular specialities. Despite his penchant for smart dark suits, good shirts and silk ties and his constant claim, as he aged, that he was merely a 'retired' businessman, Arthur was a particularly menacing figure. Les Brown, one of the city's most famous detectives, told me that no criminal he had ever met – and he met many – had the frightening hatred for the police that shone from old Arthur's cold eyes. Thompson Sr mixed with the Krays in London and with other heavies throughout the land.

He even sent some of his young henchmen for a spell at what could be described as 'finishing school', working with and studying the methods of the tough men of London's East-End gangs. On one occasion, a London contact rang to tell Arthur Sr to let his boys know that 'dead men don't pay protection money'. It never pays to underestimate the hardness of the hard men who swim in the dark waters of Glasgow's underworld. Clearly some of Thompson's neds had been a touch too anxious to show how hard they were, no doubt the better to impress Arthur himself, who was fearless, even in the company of the Krays and other gangsters such as Mad Frankie Fraser.

Here you can see squad cars outside the Ponderosa blocking the street. Vans and armed policemen are everywhere and, although not visible in this shot, a helicopter is noisily churning the murky sky overhead. This was a breakfast-time raid on the old gangster's home-turned-fortress in 1991. It lasted three hours. Officers crouched behind walls, their handguns trained on the house, while others carried out a search inside it. All this dramatic action came shortly after Arthur Jr was gunned down in the street in a still-unsolved murder.

Thompson made many enemies and he survived several assassination attempts to die in his bed from natural causes aged sixty-two. This was his car after a bomb was planted in it. His mother-in-law was killed in the blast but he escaped with his life.

Old Arthur's heir, Arthur Jr, aka 'Fatboy' or 'The Mars Bar Kid' did time on drug charges. While briefly back on the streets on short-term release from jail, he was gunned down in the street and murdered. Here, in collar and tie, he is being led away to start a sentence.

During its long reign of terror in the city, the gang gradually changed its style. At first, there was little drug dealing. Arthur's son, also Arthur but known as Fatboy, was instrumental in a switch in operations for the Thompson outfit. Young Arthur, not a patch on his father in the hard-man stakes, learned from his contacts in the south that the real money was in the import and sale of hard drugs and the gang gradually moved in that direction. He soon fell foul of the law, however, and ended up behind bars on drugs charges although, till the end, old Arthur trumpeted his belief that Fatboy, or the Mars Bar Kid as some called him, was stitched up by the cops just because of who he was – heir to a gangland empire.

Whatever the truth, young Arthur ended up blasted to death in Provanmill Road, not far from the Ponderosa. He had been on a home visit on temporarily release from prison. His night had started well with a visit to one of Glasgow's many top-class curry shops but it ended with three .22 shots in the dark – one grazed his cheek, the others entered his back and one found its way to his heart.

Paul Ferris, once a family friend of the Thompsons, ended up in court, in March 1992, charged with the murder of Fatboy and a selection of violence and drugs offences. Ferris 'walked' as they say, cleared of all charges in a famous and long-running trial – at fifty-four days, the longest murder trial in Scottish criminal history.

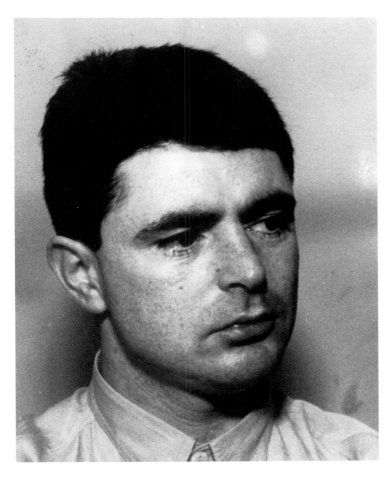

Maybe Glasgow's hard men spend too much time in cinemas or in front of TV because their criminal antics often have a Hollywood Mafia movie flavour – and never more so than on the morning of Arthur Jr's funeral. This is Bobby Glover, an east-end player on the gang scene, who was found dead in a car hours before Fatboy's final journey to the cemetery.

Dead in the car with Glover was fellow underworld name Joe 'Bananas' Hanlon. Like Glover's, his body was riddled with bullets. They had clearly displeased someone in the underworld.

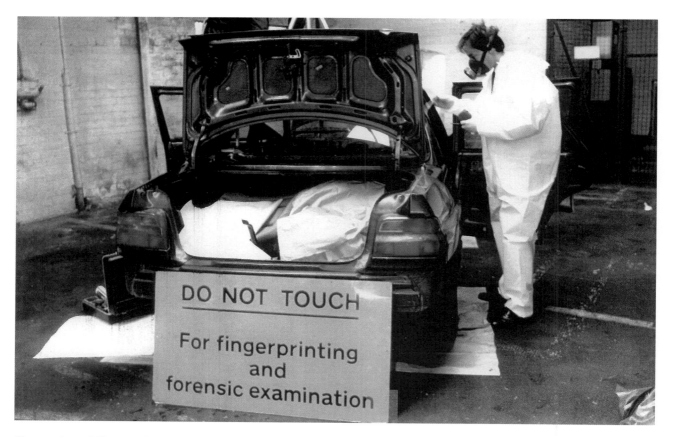

DO NOT TOUCH

For fingerprinting
and
forensic examination

The murders of Glover and Hanlon were seen as retribution for the killing of Arthur Jr and they led to the police briefing the press on a potentially deadly outbreak of armed gang-warfare. Here the forensic boys search the Ford Orion where the victims' bodies were found for clues.

The car was found outside the Cottage Bar on the corner of Darleith Street. Glover owned the pub and the Thompson funeral cortege was due to pass along the street a few hours later. The spot had obviously been chosen with care.

Arthur Jr's coffin leaves the Ponderosa for nearby Riddrie Park cemetery. As noted city crime writer Reg McKay observed, 'In more ways than one, the Thompsons spent their lives close to death'!

But, before the trial, there was another nod in the direction of Hollywood. Young Arthur's funeral was orchestrated like scenes in a Mafia film – tough-looking men and women mourning, a procession of highly polished black limos decked with flowers and undercover police mingling with the hard-faced crowds who lined the streets and gathered at the cemetery, spotting the underworld characters there to pay respect to the son of the Last Godfather. But, on top of this, there was a sensational twist to young Arthur's send-off.

Among the charges of which Ferris was cleared was one of 'murdering Arthur Thompson Jr in 1991 while acting with Robert Glover and Joseph Hanlon'. On the morning of Fatboy's funeral, Bobby Glover and Joe 'Bananas' Hanlon were found dead in a car. Both had been major players in the east-end crime scene. Glover had been given bail shortly before the murder of Fatboy after an incident in which a man was kneecapped. Hanlon was reputed to have been a strong-arm man for the drug runners known as the Barlanark Team.

The killings sparked theories galore – some said it was old Arthur's revenge. No one was charged. But it was a dramatic finale to the reign of the Thompson clan – truly worthy of Hollywood.

Here, Joe Beltrami, the legendary 'Great Defender', is pictured outside the High Court. Arthur Thompson Sr was a client for more than thirty years and provided Joe with opportunities in abundance to show his famous skills as a pleader.

There was another face to Arthur Thompson apart from the one you see in a police mug shot. He liked good clothes, dressed well and spent much time socialising at city events where his notoriety got him that staple on the menu of every gangster – respect. He had, as they say, good connections 'down south', keeping company with the likes of the Kray Twins and mixing with their crowd who also liked to party – as this shot with *Carry On* star Barbara Windsor clearly shows.

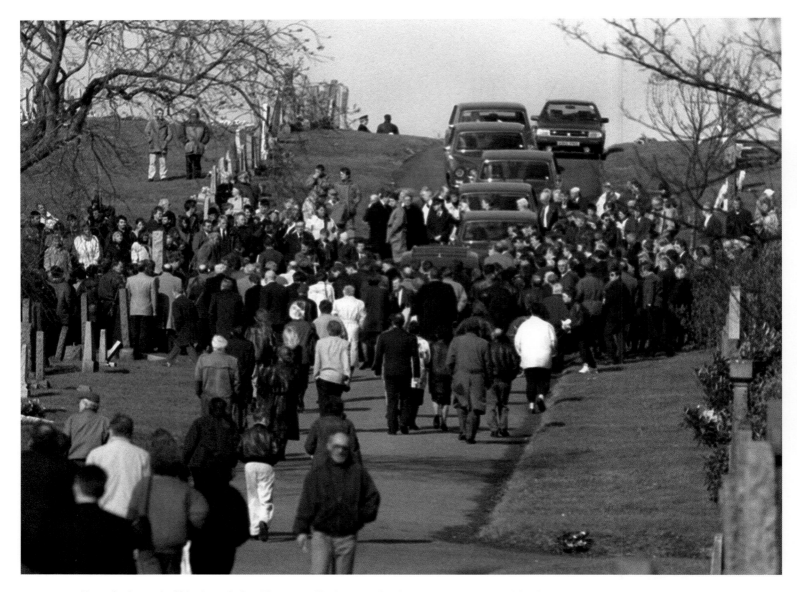

Towards the end of his days, Arthur Thompson liked to say that he was simply a retired businessman but he got a send-off that would have done a Mafia don proud. He was laid to rest in Riddrie Park cemetery near his son Fatboy in 1993. There was a police guard and florists had a field day.

This is the Last Godfather in his prime wearing a neat shirt and collar and tie but the uniform of respectability didn't really fit. Arthur was a fearsome criminal hard man who, for years, ran the east-end crime scene and grew wealthy on the profits his violence squeezed out of it.

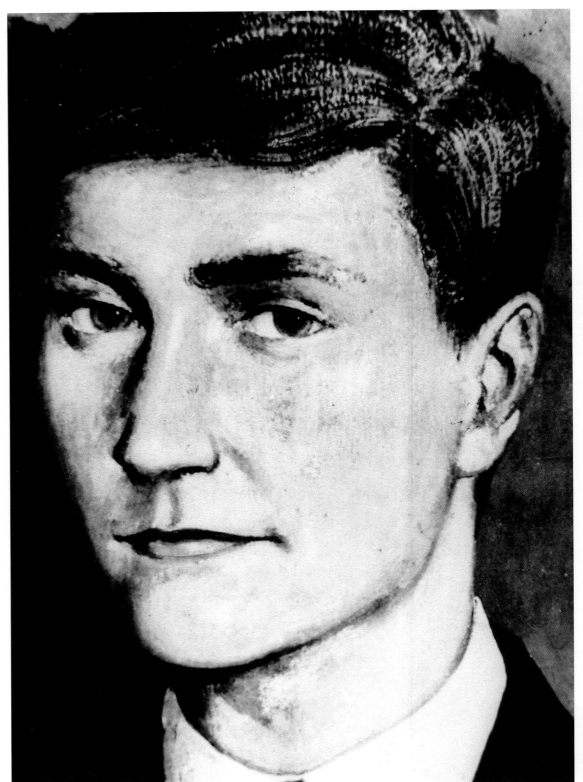

The face a city can never forget –
this is the artist's impression
drawing of Bible John that appeared
in the newspapers, on TV and
anywhere there was a chance for
the public to see it and perhaps
point the police in the right
direction. During Scotland's biggest
murder hunt, more than 100
detectives worked on the case and
50,000 statements were taken but,
almost forty years later, the murders
of Pat Docker, Mima McDonald and
Helen Puttock remain unsolved. Now
there is serious doubt about
whether or not the three murders
were committed by one person so,
like many artist's impressions, that
famous, unforgettable face may just
be an imaginative impression that is
far from reality. However, one
person who might well have been in
Bible John's company claimed it as
accurate.

CHAPTER SEVEN

Bible John: Who Was He? Did He Exist?

The horrific murders of three young 'dancing-daft' girls in Glasgow in 1968 and 1969 form one of the most enduring mysteries in the criminal past of the city. Almost forty years on, the unsolved case has taken on a new twist. The question now being asked is, 'Did Bible John exist?' At the time there was the assumption by police, press and public that there was a serial killer on the loose. Everyone knew what the hunted man looked like. In a move that was an innovative at the time, the artist's impression was everywhere, showing a clean-cut young man with close-cropped auburn or sandy hair. Even today, if you show the artist's impression of the suspect to folk of a certain age, they will identify him unhesitatingly as Bible John – no question. It is a face the city can't forget. And that, perhaps, is part of the problem.

Down the years, the ongoing hunt for Bible John has taken many an unexpected turn. The case has never been completely closed and, year after year, the newspapers turned up new leads, new theories. To find a new angle was a challenge to any

aspiring young crime reporter and many rose to it, studying the case in detail, following up old leads and applying their imagination to an intriguing case. But all the battering of typewriters and word processors, all the footslogging around the scene-of-crime sites, added nothing to solving the mystery.

Until recent years, there seemed no doubt that the three unsolved murders were the work of one man. There were similarities in the killings. The girls all died after a night at the dancing in the city's most famous hall, Barrowland, not far from Glasgow Cross. They had all been raped and strangled and the bodies had been dumped near their homes. All were known to have left the dance hall in the company of a personable young man. There were other clues to suggest the work of one man. The first victim was Pat Docker, an attractive young Langside girl who worked as an auxiliary nurse at the old Mearnskirk hospital, now the site of upmarket flats and houses. The first detectives to investigate found some disturbing aspects to the case. The raped girl had been menstruating and a

This is an archive shot of Barrowland Ballroom, one of many venues where the dancing-daft Glaswegians of the late sixties would flock. This was a place where young girls thronged to quickstep under glittering lights to the throb of a big band with the hope of maybe finding a little romance in their sometimes-drab lives. For three fans of 'a night at the Barrowland, their evenings at the 'jigging' were to end in tragedy as they were raped and strangled by a perverted killer.

sanitary towel had been placed on her body. This was to provide a link with the other two killings.

The next death attributed to Bible John was that of Jemima McDonald, who at thirty-two was seven years older than Pat Docker. She was a single mother of three children and so keen on dancing that she had been to the Barrowland on the Thursday and Friday as well as the fatal Saturday of the week she was killed. Her sister used to babysit for her so that she could go and enjoy her nights out – respite from a hard life. Like many a woman of her era and area, she wore curlers, even on a night out, covered by the ubiquitous headscarf, of course! Shortly before midnight, she was seen by fellow dancers in the company of a man, with auburn hair, in a well-cut suit, and later she was reportedly also seen in London Road with a man, probably the same guy, whose appearance, according to the newspapers, vaguely matched the description of Bible John. Even later, she was seen with a man on derelict property near her home in McKeith Street. This was the last time she was seen alive.

On the Monday morning, she was found lying face down on the floor of a condemned ground-floor flat. Her coat had been half pulled off and her shoes were not on her feet. Her tights had been removed and were torn. She had been strangled and had injuries to head and face. The similarities in the two killings were emerging – Pat Docker's body also had face and head injuries and, although her shoes were still on, her outer clothing had been torn off. And Mima, as she was known, had, like Pat, been menstruating. It looked like Bible John had struck again. But little was made of one fact

that has subsequently taken on more significance – Jemima McDonald died all of eighteen months after Pat Docker.

There was not to be such a long gap between the second and third killings. The next victim of the so-called Bible John – a man now firmly embedded in the consciousness of Glasgow police and public – was twenty-nine-year-old Helen Puttock, who died in October 1969. During reports of the earlier murders, the police had briefed the city's crime reporters that the suspect was probably called John and that, on occasion, he spoke of a strict upbringing and of a family seemingly averse to the drinking culture of the time and that he often mentioned the Bible. It was a short step from this for top crime reporter John Quinn to suggest to his news editor that the mysterious killer should be referred to as Bible John. The name stuck and was taken up by all the newspapers, radio and television.

When Helen Puttock was found dead, face down, with head injuries and strangled by her torn clothing, there was the immediate assumption that Bible John had struck again. At the time, the similarities where enough to convince both police and public that all the killings were the work of one man. It seems, looking back, that no consideration was given to the possibility of one or other of the murders being copycat killings. One good reason for this is that many of the details of the similarities were known only to the police and had not been revealed in the millions of words written about the case. But, as any student of true crime knows, such details can still leak out and end up in the wrong hands. There are fewer secrets in a murder inquiry than you might expect. The Helen Puttock killing

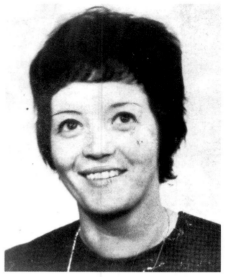

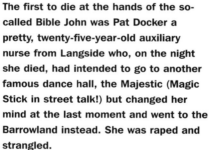

The first to die at the hands of the so-called Bible John was Pat Docker a pretty, twenty-five-year-old auxiliary nurse from Langside who, on the night she died, had intended to go to another famous dance hall, the Majestic (Magic Stick in street talk!) but changed her mind at the last moment and went to the Barrowland instead. She was raped and strangled.

Thirty-two-year-old Mima McDonald, who lived in MacKeith Street, not far from the London Road ballroom, was so keen on her night outs that, on the weekend of her death, she had been there on the Thursday and Friday as well the Saturday. Victim number two, she was raped and strangled in August 1969, eighteen months after Pat Docker had died.

The final victim was Helen Puttock, a twenty-nine-year-old who had gone dancing with her sister Jeannie. After a taxi ride from the city back to her home in Scotstoun, Helen, too, ended up raped and strangled. This time, however, there was to be a good description of the killer as Jeannie had been in the taxi with Helen and her new 'friend', a man called John. Jeannie told the police that the artist's impression poster of Bible John was remarkably like the man who had shared the taxi with the sisters.

The *Daily Record*, a redtop tabloid still much given to following the happenings in gangland, produced a poster to aid the hunt for the Barrowland monster.

Senior police officers leave the scene of Pat Docker's murder, a lane near her south-side home, on 24 February 1968.

had one important difference from the others. This time there was a good witness. Jeannie, Helen's sister, was in the Barrowland with her that night and she had met the man Helen danced with. He was well dressed, with auburn hair, and on a taxi ride home, he spoke of the Bible! Jeannie was able to give a detailed description and it has to be said it matched the artist's impression remarkably closely.

One strange aspect of the case is the number of Glaswegians picked up by the cops on the grounds that they were dead ringers for the artist's impression poster! All were released. And even a suspect, arrested near the Barrowland in suspicious circumstances, was freed when detectives found he didn't have a distinctive dental defect that was an important part of the official Bible John description. That was enough to rule him out.

The facts are that more than 100 detectives worked on the case. Almost half a million statements were taken. Unsolved murders have a gripping fascination. The mysteries they pose refuse to die. In 1996, twenty-eight years after Pat Docker slipped into her dancing best for a night under the bright lights of Barrowland, there was a particularly macabre twist to the tale. John McInnes, a furniture salesman who committed suicide in 1980, had at

WOMAN FOUND
IN BACK COURT

POLICE
CARAVAN

SCOTSTOUN
TERMINUS

WOMAN'S
HOUSE

TO DUMBARTON
ROAD

The newspapers of the day liked to run this sort of labelled shot alongside big stories and crime reporters and photographers would help the retouchers create them with enthusiasm. Helen Puttock was found in the backcourt of a block of flats just 150 yards from her home.

one time been a suspect but he was eliminated when he was not picked out at an identity parade. But suspicion lingered and the advances in DNA testing led to his grave being broken open on a cold February day and his remains taken to the lab for testing. There was nothing to match traces of semen that had been found on the third body and five months later he was officially cleared.

But perhaps the last word should come from Joe Beattie, the detective who spent years leading the hunt. In a final interview with *The Herald*, not long before he died, he mentioned lingering doubts that one man had killed all three girls. And the

evidence of the lives of other multi-murderers, I believe, supports him. Serial killers, by their nature, tend not leave eighteen-month gaps between the deaths of their victims. Could it be that the almost obsessive belief that all the killings were down to one man flawed the investigations, stopping other lines of inquiry and ruling out the possibility that there was more than one killer?

If each murder had been investigated totally separately, not in the context of the Bible John publicity machine, would there have been a different ending to Glasgow's greatest mystery? I think so.

The interviews of everyone with a connection, how ever remote, to a murder investigation are painstakingly recorded. Here a detective consults his clipboard which has a picture of Mina McDonald on it to jog memories.

Detectives gather at the lane where Pat Docker's naked body was discovered. The investigation found some disturbing aspects to the case. One was the fact that the young nurse had been menstruating and a sanitary towel had been carefully placed on her body – something that this murder was to have in common with the McDonald and Puttock killings.

BIBLE JOHN —NEW HUNT

EXCLUSIVE

Triple murder probe reopens after tip-off

THE 15-year-old Bible John mystery took a sensational turn today.

For police have been given information that the Glasgow killer may be alive and living in Holland.

The dramatic tip-off came from a Glasgow private detective. It has triggered off the first major move in the case for more than a decade.

It was in 1968 that Bible John claimed his first victim — a pretty young nurse whose naked body was dumped in a lane. The following year two more young women were killed after nights out at Glasgow's Barrowland dance hall.

Now the files have been reopened as two top detectives who were involved in the original inquiries probe the new tip-off.

They have been told that a friend of the private detective knows the suspect personally.

Today Glasgow's Procurator Fiscal James Todhope confirmed that police are making new investigations into the Bible John killings.

He said: "Our office is assisting the police with their inquiries into this matter.

"We provided them with a number of our files on the case.

"They include precognitions and statements.

"There is no question of extradition papers being asked for. The inquiry is at an early stage."

By MIKE HILDREY

Since the fresh tip-off, witnesses who were questioned at the time of the killings have been re-interviewed.

Detective Superintendent James Brown, now stationed at Paisley, said: "I am one of the few remaining serving officers who was involved in the case.

Asked about the new development, he said: "I have been to the Procurator-Fiscal. These allegations crop up from time to time."

The suspect is said to have been living in Holland for several years.

He is a Scot, believed to be from Glasgow, who was living in the city at the time of the killings.

A picture of the suspect has been supplied to the police.

It shows a man aged between 19 and 23, taken years ago.

It is understood that an artist has been called in to "age" the picture.

BIBLE JOHN . . . the face that brought terror to Glasgow

DANCE OF DEATH — PAGES 2 AND 3

INSIDE: WEATHER: 2 NEWS: 2,3,4,5,9,13,15,17,18,21,27,30 DIARY, LETTERS: 6 LOOK: 10,11 TV EXTRA: 23,24,25,26

Down the years, the hunt for Bible John has been re-opened whenever a new snippet of information has emerged. This is how the *Evening Times* reported one such inquiry. Like others it failed to solve the mystery.

Public interest in the hunt for Bible John was almost insatiable. Here the crime reporters crowd in on the incident caravan to get the latest snippet from Detective Joe Beattie.

Beattie was a pivotal figure in the inquiry. Here (second left), he discusses the case with fellow detectives under an identikit picture of their quarry.

This is John McInnes. During the original investigation, suspicion had, at one time, fallen on him – he committed suicide in 1980, not long after Helen Puttock's death. At the time, detectives ruled him out but, in 1996, in one of the frequent re-examinations of the case, his body was exhumed and taken away for DNA testing.

Police officers take the coffin of John McInnes away from the grave-diggers' tent in a snowy Stonehouse cemetery to await DNA testing. The final result took some months but it showed that he had not killed Helen Puttock and the Crown announced that he was completely cleared. The mystery of who Bible John was or whether he even existed remains.

Samuel 'Dandy' McKay was a bank robber and prison escape artist whose antics, as reported regularly in the papers, made him one of the best-known villains in the city in the sixties and seventies. He and a man named Alex Gray had carried off one of the biggest bank robberies, the famous Shettleston job, by the simple method of acquiring a key, walking in and collecting a large amount of readies – clever but, as they got caught, not clever enough! And Dandy, so-called because of his passion for neat dress, got ten years for that one. He escaped and fled to Canada where he was arrested and taken back to Scotland – and promptly made another escape. The papers had him down as a cross between the Scarlet Pimpernel and Robin Hood.

CHAPTER EIGHT

A Cop Killer and Hard Cases with Nothing to Lose

Down the years, Glasgow may have written its name large in the history of gangs and gang fighting but it also had a hard bunch whose interests were much more commercial than the bloody battles of sectarian mobs or wild teenagers engaging in turf wars or cutting up rivals. In the days before you needed an honours degree in information technology to rob a bank, the city spawned a succession of legendary characters – armed robbers who specialised in large unauthorised withdrawals from the toughest of safes, mostly outside office hours. These included the 'King of the Twilight Zone', Walter Norval, Walter Scott Ellis and Dandy McKay.

For a spell in the fifties and sixties, Dandy's exploits filled the tabloids. In his day, the average hood dressed in ill-fitting slacks, a ragged sports jacket and beer-stained tie. Not Mr McKay – he liked smart suits and well-cut shirts and any booze or food stains that might have been picked up in pub planning sessions resulted in a trip to the dry-cleaners. The Glasgow criminal fraternity are strong on nicknames but little ingenuity in this area

was expended on Samuel McKay. That he was known in law-breaking circles as Dandy is, as they say, a no-brainer.

Those who knew him well will tell you that he could look after himself but he was not a man to use violence lightly. Like a lot of criminals of his type, he had his own set of rules – a criminal code of conduct. If force was required, it was used but only if necessary. Dandy was often to be found in banks and houses where he had no right of entry but, unlike one of Scotland's most infamous killers, Peter Manuel, he did not believe in killing the occupants. In fact, Peter Manuel's crimes angered many of the old school of professional criminals who were keeping the cops busy with their payroll robberies, bank break-ins and burglaries. They wanted him caught.

McKay was no different and, when Manuel tried to implicate him in his killings, he was particularly angry. The cops knew Dandy too well to listen to the ramblings of the evil Lanarkshire killer. But McKay knew a bit about Manuel himself and, outraged by what was going on, as the serial killer spread fear through the city, he cooperated in nailing him. He told the police all he knew of Peter Manuel, including dates and times and other pieces of vital evidence that would help send him to the gallows.

It was not the only time he aided the police. Les Brown, one of the city's legendary detectives, tells of his relationship with McKay in *Glasgow Crimefighter* by Les Brown and Robert Jeffrey (Black & White, Edinburgh, 2005). The bank robber used a secret code to contact the detective and they would take a walk in the park where little nuggets of information, helpful to the police, were dropped into the conversation. Unsurprisingly, those named in these undercover jaunts were no friends of Samuel McKay. McKay added to his lustre as a headline provoker with his famed ability as a successful jail breaker.

In the fifties, another infamous bank robber was also making headlines – and influencing how they were written. Walter Scott Ellis had a major effect on the reporting of crime in Scotland when he was cleared of a murder charge. The press fought – literally – to get his story when he emerged from court. This unseemly scrum resulted in changes that apply to this day in the way court cases are reported. Later Scott Ellis ended up in Peterhead, where he had Walter Norval for company, for a bank robbery conducted with John 'Bat' Neeson and James McIntyre aka

Les Brown was a controversial city detective around the time McKay was making headlines. He struck up a relationship with Dandy that could have come straight out of spy fiction. McKay would phone Brown and ask him the colour of his dog. Les would reply, 'Red.' and the caller replied, 'Mine is black.' That was the prompt for a meet in Linn Park, near both their homes. There, some titbit from the underworld that it suited McKay to divulge would be dropped in the detective's ear.

Any cop killer is truly hated by the men in blue who risk their lives on daily basis to keep law and order but, when the killer has himself once been a police officer, the hatred ratchets up even more. Howard Wilson, seen here in 1970 about to start a long sentence, was such a reviled figure. Wilson left the force after a failed career and started a new one as a bank robber but he was no more successful at that than he was as a cop. After a raid, he was tracked to his home in Allison Street, just off Victoria Road, and, as the police moved in, he shot two officers dead and injured a third.

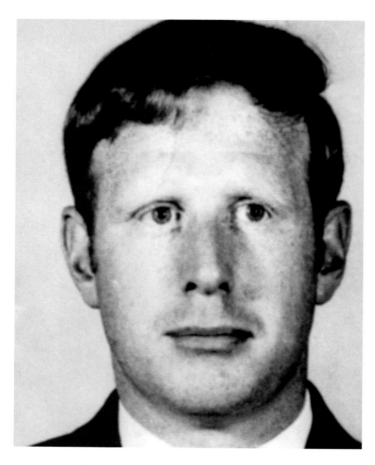

Detective Constable Angus McKenzie, shot by Howard Wilson.

Detective Edward Barnett, the other officer killed by Wilson.

'Mac the Knife'. Neeson's nickname was a nod in the direction of his bad eyesight, not a reflection of his ability with that oft-used Glasgow weapon of coercion, the baseball bat.

In the sixties, another horrific crime made its mark on the city's history. Gangsters fight gangsters, cornered burglars can kill householders to escape the scene of their crime but, for the police, there is one villain reviled above all – a cop killer. And, when a cop or ex-cop kills his own, the reaction is dramatic. In 1969, Allison Street, just off Victoria Road, became the scene of one of the city's most notorious double murders. The killer was a former police inspector, Howard Wilson. He had left the force soured by lack of promotion – maybe a wise move by his superiors – and opened a greengrocer's in Allison Street. This loser was soon in debt and got the notion to join two other members of a gun club and start a new career as a bank robber. Like his police career and that in commerce, it too ended in failure. A raid on a bank in Linwood was ill thought-out and led to them being spotted on their return to Wilson's flat. He had unwisely set up house just round the corner from Craigie Street police station, an area full of cops coming and going to their work. And many of them knew Wilson. In a police raid on the flat, the cornered cop killed Detective Constable Angus McKenzie and PC Edward Barnett. Inspector Andrew Hyslop was injured but survived. The services for the killed policemen who had died bravely in the course of duty showed the depth of the revulsion shared by police and public and brought thousands on to the streets. The man who pulled the trigger served thirty-two years in jail.

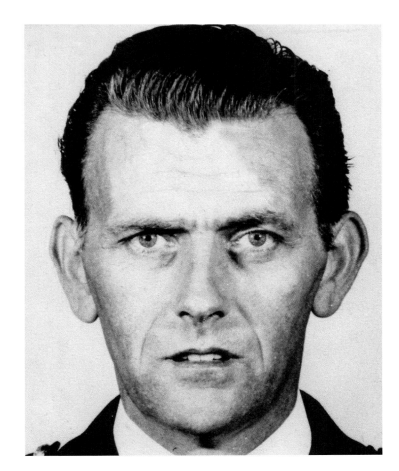

Although injured in the Allison Street shoot-out, Inspector Andrew Hyslop survived and resumed his police career, at one point lecturing young policemen on firearms.

This is the gun, a Vostok .22 target pistol made in the USSR, that Howard Wilson used to kill two police officers and injure a third.

Huge crowds turned out on the streets to watch as a massive contingent of mourning colleagues of Angus McKenzie and Edward Barnett marched up High Street. Led by the police pipe band, they are on their way to the Eastern Necropolis.

Floral tributes, uniformed police and tears at the rain-soaked funeral of Edward Barnett who was killed on duty.

Grim-faced officers line the approaches to Linn Park cemetery as the coffin of Angus McKenzie is taken to its last resting place.

This is cop killer Howard Wilson, who was released after more than thirty years in jail.

The bag over the head is a common manoeuvre on police office steps. In this 1959 photo, the man hidden from the cameras is a seventeen–year-old butcher's boy from Cambuslang who was accused of killing a female shopkeeper. The dapper figure second from the left is Chief Detective Super Robert Colquhoun, a well-kent face on the police scene at the time.

In those days, the curious thronged around police stations where suspects in infamous cases were detained. This crowd was outside Lawmuir Street station where the youth accused of the murder of a shopkeeper was held. It is striking how many young children gathered on such occasions.

The murdered shopkeeper, Mrs Helen McGhee, worked in this shop in Cathcart Road, Mount Florida.

The debate about the role played by slum upbringings in criminality still rages today. The leafy suburbs can produce criminals of all stripes but there is no doubt the Gorbals of old spawned more than its share of evildoers. This famous image from the *Herald/Times* archive is remarkable in that it captures the look of slum streets of the twenties and thirties but it was taken as recently as 1964.

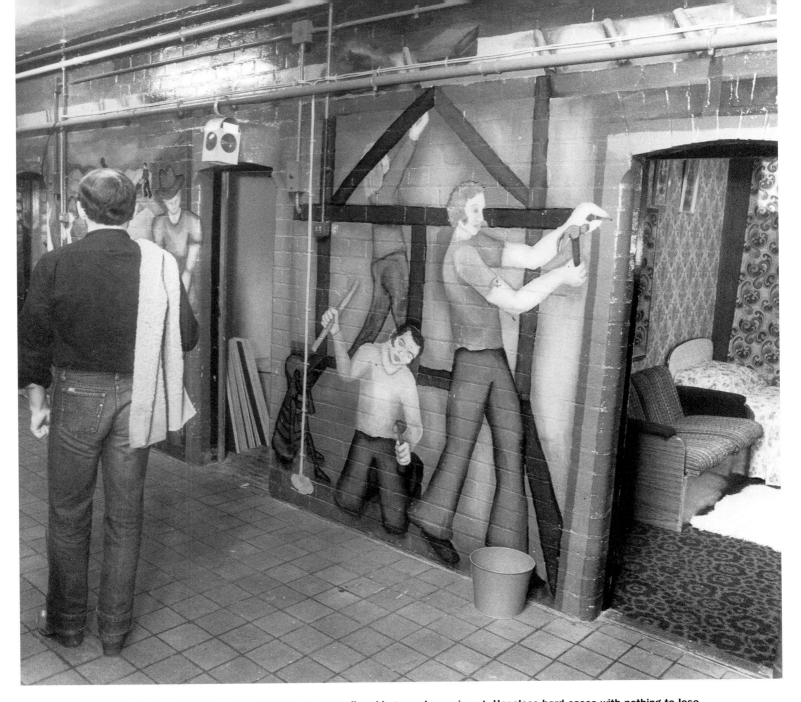

The Barlinnie Special Unit was a world-famous, groundbreaking penal experiment. Hopeless hard cases with nothing to lose were causing mayhem in conventional jails so a select few were moved to the Special Unit, where they were taught creative writing, sculpture and painting and treated like human beings rather than caged animals. This shot gives a flavour of what the place was like in 1981. Eventually it ran out of steam and was closed after lurid tales involving smuggled drugs and sex behind bars. But it forever altered penal policy in Scotland and many of the advances made there were adopted in conventional jails.

Hugh Collins, here in reflective mood, is one of the success stories of the unit. On release, he expressed regret at the crime that had seen him imprisoned and he subsequently rebuilt his life, becoming a successful sculptor and sensitive writer.

Another man changed by the challenges that the Special Unit offered its inmates was James Boyle, who also went down the route of sculpture and the arts and ended up with a new life as a Rolls Royce owner and wine buff. In public, at least, he seemed less able than Collins to apologise for his crimes and to handle criticism of his new life. In one interview he attacked those who grudged him his material success head-on, saying, 'The only thing I can say about people like that is that they have allowed themselves to become prisoners of my past.'

When in Peterhead, Jimmy Boyle was infamous for his dirty protests and, for a time, the far north-east fortress seemed to have a permanent population on the prison roof throwing slates down on the 'screws' below. Barlinnie has had similar moments, most spectacularly when Sammy 'The Bear' Ralston claimed in 1987 that he had been assaulted by warders and the inmates took to the roof with hostages. Menacing hooded figures with weapons, they are seen here silhouetted high on the Bar-L's roof.

Here, angry Barlinnie prisoners, risking life and limb to make their point, put on quite a show for TV and the newspapers. Three years later, long after peace had been restored to the Bar-L, a sheriff ruled that Ralston had not been assaulted.

This book would not exist without the dedication of newspaper photographers. Here is the press corps en masse with their long lenses targeted on the Bar-L roof, ready to catch the next moves in a real-life drama. Among the snappers are two respected figures in the trade, Brian Fair and Alistair Devine, and, for once, they are the subject themselves.

This is Paddy Meehan, who was unjustly convicted of the murder of Rachel Ross in Ayr in 1969. Like Oscar Slater's before him, his case attracted the attention of the press and literary figures and he was eventually pardoned. Meehan was a non-violent minor Glasgow crook and safebreaker who had the bad luck to be convicted as a result of a flawed identity parade.

CHAPTER NINE

An Innocent Man in the Dock, Yet Again

The Glaswegian takes what some might call an unhealthy interest in the doings of the bad guys. The preponderance of detailed crime reports and speculation in the city's lively crop of newspapers, both tabloid and broadsheet, prove that. And, if you ask anyone in pub or office to name the current crop of villains who despoil the city, they will come up with a handful of names before you can pull out a notebook or take the first sip of your pint. The armchair pundits seldom come face to face with the men who make the headlines on the crime pages but the case of Paddy Meehan is an exception. The man who suffered perhaps the greatest injustice since Oscar Slater met more of the public than any underworld figure before or since. For the commuters in railway and bus stations and folk who walked the city streets during his final years, before his death in 1994, Meehan was a tragic figure accosting strangers and urging them to buy his book, a bizarre tome called *Framed by MI5*. To an extent, however, he seemed to enjoy his notoriety and loved sharing a drink with journalists or anyone he met in the pub with the price of a pint and the time to listen to his tale. And, finally out of jail for a murder he did not commit, he had a brief career on the right side of the law advising on home security!

As everyone knew, Meehan was free to pound the city-centre pavements hawking his literary wares, rather than rotting in solitary in Peterhead, mainly due to a campaign led by Joe Beltrami, Ludovic Kennedy, David Scott and others. But Meehan's book was largely devoted to his feud with Beltrami in the years after his conviction – though it did also postulate the unlikely notion that he was a victim of a secret-service plot concocted to silence him with regard to what he described as his role in the escape of Soviet spy George Blake from a London prison in 1966. Ironically Joe, the Great Defender, was responsible for Paddy having to be his own salesman. Joe – who had written a splendid book on the case himself, *A Deadly Innocence* – took exception to what Meehan was saying in his book and threatened a major bookshop with legal action if they stocked it. Others steered clear of this dangerous book as well and it ended up sold on the

James Griffiths, an utter no-good from Lancashire, had teamed up with Meehan on a series of robberies and the pair had passed through Ayr on the night of Rachael Ross's murder. Police went to Griffiths' house to quiz him and a bloody shoot-out resulted. He fled through the city streets in a commandeered car and shot a newsvendor, spraying bullets as he fled. Eventually, he was shot down by the police when cornered in a west-end flat.

streets by the author himself, in the tradition of the famous Glasgow pamphleteers of the past.

But all this was long, sensation-filled years after the great injustice of Meehan's conviction in the autumn of 1969. Rachael Ross, a pensioner, lived in bungalow in Ayr with her ex-bookmaker husband Abraham, who had a bingo business in Paisley. The underworld knew there was a fair chance of money lurking in a safe in the Ross home. In those days, cash from an enterprise conducted when the banks were closed could take a day or two to be lodged. The west of Scotland was truly shocked by what happened to the old couple. It was a horrendous murder. Intruders broke into their home and tied up the couple while they looked for cash. Mrs Ross was horribly bludgeoned round the head and, when the intruders made their escape, both she and her husband were left alone, cruelly and painfully tied up and unable to move. The Ross's lay injured and undetected for many long hours, their shouts for help going unheard, and were only discovered when a cleaning lady arrived on the morning of the Monday after their weekend assault.

Abraham survived the ordeal but Mrs Ross died in hospital from her injuries. It had been a brutal business and the details of the merciless attack shocked newspaper readers, who were no strangers to the ugly details of crime. The pressure was on the cops. And, as is often the case, their first stop was to call on the usual suspects. Paddy Meehan had no real record of violence though he was an experienced housebreaker and peterman. And it turned out he had been in the area on the night of the murder. He had passed through Ayr, on the way from a recce of a motor taxation office in Stranraer that he planned to turn over in company with a criminal colleague, Englishman Jim Griffiths. Two and two were added up, not for the first time in the annals of Glasgow crime, to provide not four but the answer the police wanted. They reckoned that Meehan and Griffiths had been responsible. Griffiths did have a record of violence. He also had an obsessive fear of being locked up.

Rachael Ross was left, battered and tied up, to die an agonising death inside this bungalow.

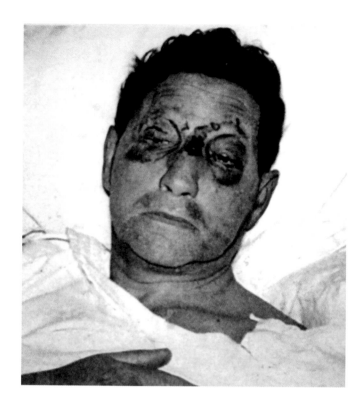

The violence used against pensioners Rachael Ross and her husband Abraham, an ex-bookie and bingo hall owner who had cash in a safe in the house, is horrifically illustrated by this shot taken in hospital as he struggled to come to terms with the death of his wife.

This is Rachael Ross who died in the Ayr break-in.

The scene inside the Rosses' bungalow after the murder.

West enders fled for cover in Great Western Road as deranged gunman James Griffiths fired indiscriminately from a tenement window.

This fear was to be the fuse that ignited a bloody and deadly spree on the streets of Glasgow. When the cops approached his home to question him about events in Ayr, Griffiths went berserk. He met them with a hail of bullets and embarked on a daylight rampage through the city. He had a rifle and a shotgun and, at one stage, he fired indiscriminately into a children's playground. He shot nine men, one fatally, two women, a child and a police officer. He holed up in flat in Springburn where he was finally shot down. It was brave work by the police that brought to an end a siege that could have cost many more lives than it did but there was a less savoury aspect to the police attitude

to the incident. With the body carted off to the morgue and the streets safe to walk again, the police announced publicly that, with Griffiths dead and Meehan under arrest, they were no longer looking for anyone else for the killing of Mrs Ross – so much for the chance of a fair trial for Patrick Connolly Meehan. That unwise announcement was to resonate down the years. But, of course, the assumption that Griffiths and Paddy were the Ayr killers, based on Griffiths's panic, was not enough alone to convict Meehan. That took a flawed identity parade and a trial that led to accusations of the police planting evidence and failing to follow lines of inquiry that didn't fit their preconceived

A bullet hole in the bay window of the flat where the Griffiths siege began.

The car in which Griffiths fled from the police lies abandoned in a lane near Oakbank Hospital.

notions on the crime. But convicted he was despite the efforts of Joe Beltrami, Nicky Fairbairn and John Smith (later to lead the Labour Party) in his defence team.

The obvious flaws in the police case and the trial led to the famous campaign to free Paddy who was in solitary for nine years and not at all a cooperative prisoner – not surprising since he was innocent. Some years after the cell door first swung shut on Meehan, Joe Beltrami heard some interesting news on the case. On several occasions, one of the Great Defender's clients, an infamous Glasgow lowlife called 'Tank' McGuinness, told Beltrami that he and another man were responsible for the Ross murder. Joe Beltrami was adamant that the solicitor–client relationship meant that he could neither investigate this claim nor make it public while McGuinness

was still alive – this was at the root of the later feud between Joe and Paddy.

But in March 1976, McGuinness was found beaten and unconscious in a Parkhead street. He died thirteen days later in the Royal – that famous Glasgow institution much used to taking in the victims of the street wars. Another notorious figure was charged with the killing – John 'Gypsy' Winning, a so-called 'friend' of Tank. He was found not guilty because of lack of evidence but was himself murdered in Fife a few years later. The other major figure in this sordid saga was Ian Waddell who was also murdered – again by a so-called 'friend', one Andrew Gentle whose name belied his nature. In the Glasgow underworld, as in ancient Rome, it pays to be wary of friends! But first Waddell was tried and cleared of killing Mrs Ross.

Customers from the Round Toll bar in Possil examine cartridges that littered the streets after the rampage.

The newspaper furore over the sensational twists and turns in the case eventually caused the then Scottish Secretary to order an inquiry under Lord Hunter. Taking five years to complete, the inquiry finally made it clear that McGuinness and Waddell were the men who broke into the bungalow and assaulted the old couple. But, shamefully, it also said it was not impossible that Meehan and Griffiths had later been used to open the safe. Ludovic Kennedy was of the opinion that the establishment's tendency to throw suspicion on Paddy any time they got the chance was intended to obscure the claims that the police were guilty of planting evidence. The Free Meehan campaign team issued a statement that any suggestion that Meehan had played any role in the crime was without evidence. As the years go by that seems clearer and clearer.

And, to my mind at least, it seems that the reckless initial statement, with Griffiths's body barely cold, that no one else was in the frame for the killing of Mrs Ross not only denied Meehan a fair trial – it was what drove the cover-up down the years.

A cop with a bandolier relays the message that the incident has ended.

Chief Constable James Robertson briefs the press at the end of the shoot-out.

Eight people had been injured and one person killed before the blanket-covered body of James Griffiths was taken to the morgue. Tom Goodall looks on as the stretcher is carried to the ambulance.

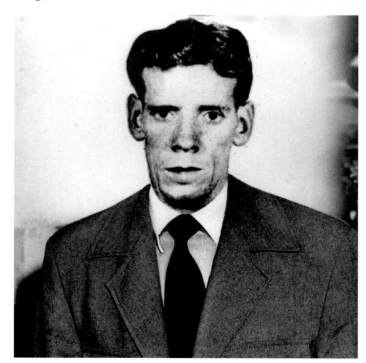

'Tank' McGuinness, an infamous Glasgow lowlife who died in a brawl, was responsible for the killing of old Mrs Ross. Significantly the underworld knew McGuinness as a notorious 'tie-up merchant'.

Ian Waddell, left, who was in the Ayr house with McGuinness, was himself murdered some years later.

On the left is Joe Beltrami on his way into the High Court with John 'Gypsy' Winning in August 1976. Winning was accused of murdering McGuinness but the charges were dropped because of lack of evidence. Winning was himself murdered in his house in Fife in 1980.

When Paddy Meehan wrote from his prison cell to Ludovic Kennedy, it was perhaps the smartest move he ever made. Kennedy was a famous campaigner against injustice and a respected national figure. A 'Free Meehan' campaign committee, which included lawyers Joe Beltrami, Ross Harper, Len Murray, David Burnside and Bert Kerrigan and respected city TV and newspaper reporter David Scott, was formed – a good team to have on your side.

The flamboyant Nicky Fairbairn was one of Meehan's original defence team – as was the late Labour leader, John Smith.

Here's a familiar scene – wet pavements, a gathering of cops in raincoats and the word on the street is out, in *Taggart* style, that 'there's been a murder'. This time, Govan and the whole city would be shocked by the McMonigle murders.

CHAPTER TEN

Death by Fire, Knife, Hammer and Gun

Crimes Past is not a story with a happy ending. Dispiriting and depressing are the adjectives that spring to mind when you consider that crime and gangs in Glasgow really took hold on the public consciousness in the final days of the nineteenth century and now, in the early years of the twenty-first, the headlines still have a familiar ring to them. In March 2006, a conference in the Royal Concert Hall was told that violence in Scotland as a whole cost an estimated £3 billion a year. The burden on the health service alone was said to be in the region of £500 million. And it is a safe bet that a significant proportion of that costly violence takes place in Glasgow. In a dramatic illustration that we have not moved all that far from the bloody days of the Redskins, the Billy Boys and the hundreds of other violent gangs of the past, the audience listened to a distinguished Accident and Emergency consultant, Michael Sheridan, who said:

> People have no idea of the consequences of their actions. This weekend I worked two 9 a.m. to 9 p.m. shifts. I dealt with a person struck on the head with a machete, another suffering knife wounds who required surgery and a third who was stabbed in the chest.

It is hard to resist the remark, 'What's new?'

Such conferences and the continuing pressure on a hard-pressed police force show just how wrong those who, down the years, have failed to face up to what was happening in their city have been. To tackle a problem you must first acknowledge it is there. And, for years, in an attempt to sweep the bad news under the carpet, some pundits and politicians have not done that. And with a predictable frequency events, as they say, make what is going on impossible to ignore. Glasgow is used to frequent sudden shocks knocking the rose-coloured spectacles off the most committed of optimists and bringing the citizenry face to face with horrible reality.

It happened once again on a bleak Saturday in January 1976. John McMonigle, a father of three children, the oldest of whom was just twelve,

In this Govan backcourt, a cop with his notebook asks some kids, who no doubt knew the young victims of a particularly horrible crime, if they can help with his inquiries.

This squad car and incident van are parked at a close-mouth. Upstairs is a scene of carnage in the blood-soaked flat, where two innocent kids lie dead.

Nowadays a spruced-up Glasgow subway glories in the nickname of The Clockwork Orange. In the mid-seventies it was a darker, grimmer place but the painstaking business of interviewing anyone who might have a lead went on, even underground.

had left his Govan home in the morning to look at new accommodation on offer in Pollok. It would have been a dream move for him and his family for they lived in a half-empty tenement that was waiting for the wreckers' ball. The few families who were left lived in terror of looters and lowlifes. It was an appalling place to live. Mr McMonigle had only taken one of his three children with him to Pollok to look at the new house offered to the family by the Corporation. This was welcome news for a father anxious to get his family settled in a new and better environment. It was a must to get to see the place on offer as soon as possible and Mr McMonigle went to Pollok by bus accompanied by his daughter Elizabeth. Young Irene and John were left playing in the street along with other local children, not uncommon in those days. On his return to Golspie Street he opened his door at teatime that Saturday to a scene from hell.

One of the first detectives to arrive after the 999 call was the legendary Les Brown. He told me, 'I have seen some horrific sights in my career but none as bad as this.' An intruder had battered the kids mercilessly with a hammer. Les said, 'It was possible to count the hammer blows from the trails of blood on the ceiling as the implement was drawn back for the next blow.' After some sound detective work – Glasgow cops have plenty of practice – a man called Alex Miller was arrested and he said he had gone to the house in the near-derelict tenement to steal a TV set and was disturbed by his two young victims. He flew into a rage and battered the two kids to death and went home to his girlfriend's flat, where he watched the end of an episode of *Dr Who* on TV.

He eventually pled guilty to two charges of

murder and was sent to Carstairs. An obsession for TV had cost two young lives.

A few years later, in 1980, Les Brown found himself embroiled in a particularly controversial murder case. This time the victim, Tracy Main, was just into her teens and the scene of crime was the Gorbals – but in a new high-rise, not an old tenement. Les made a spectacular mistake in this intriguing case. He is commendably upfront about this disaster and tells the tale in full in his autobiography, *Glasgow Crimefighter* (Black & White, Edinburgh 2005) The young girl had been stabbed to death in the family house at Norfolk Court and suspicion fell on a man who stayed with a neighbour. He went to trial in the High Court but the case collapsed when it emerged that Les Brown had made a mistake in administering the caution during the charging procedures. The charge was dropped and the accused released.

Murders like that of the McMonigle kids and young Tracy Main become huge talking points. But often the public memory is short and, after a few years, details of the cases drift into the criminal shadows, only remembered by the families, the police, lawyers and reporters involved. But the murder of the Doyle family in Bankend Street, Ruchazie, in spring 1984, marked the start of a legal saga that was to run for more than twenty years. The everyday details of it became familiar to millions. The Ice-Cream Wars and the wrongful imprisonment of big TC Campbell and Joe Steele for fire bombing the Doyles' flat were seldom out of the headlines in all that time. Back in the eighties the ice-cream vans running around the bleak estates of post-war Glasgow made big money. Substances

Here an officer is conducting door-to-door inquires, a police tactic that can be surprisingly successful.

Gorbals high-rise flats brought a new life to many families freed from the misery of the old tenements. For the Main family, they brought tragedy.

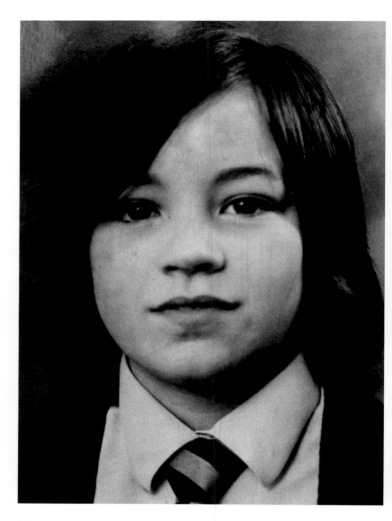

This is Tracy Main who was murdered in her home.

more dangerous to health than ice cream or even cigarettes were sometimes involved though there was big business for legitimate traders too.

The saga started as a fairly run-of-the-mill Friday night/Saturday morning Glasgow fire story in the early editions of the *Evening Times*. But the casualty list grew quickly and it was soon clear that the blaze had been started deliberately and sinister motives began to emerge. Those who died were: James Doyle Sr (53), James Doyle Jr (23), Tony Doyle (14), Andrew Doyle (18), their sister Christine Halleron (25) and her baby Mark. The investigating cops established that the fire had been started in a cupboard used for storing tyres and timber, a dangerous combination, and the flames

which exploded out of the cupboard flashed through the flat with deadly speed. They also found that young Andrew's career as an ice-cream van salesman had previously exposed him to danger – on one occasion, shots had been fired at his van and, on another, he had been beaten up outside his home. It was a vendetta. The heavies were moving in on the ice-cream business.

In first of many court appearances, TC Campbell, who had run with the infamous Goucho gang, and Thomas Lafferty had been accused of attempting to murder Andrew Doyle and fifteen-year-old Anne Wilson, who helped on the rounds, by firing a shot at them through the windscreen of their ice-cream van. Other charges involved

This is the fire-blackened exterior of the Doyles' flat in Bankend Street on a dreich day when the weather matched the feeling of the folk in Ruchazie and throughout the city. TC Campbell and Joe Steele were convicted of setting the fire.

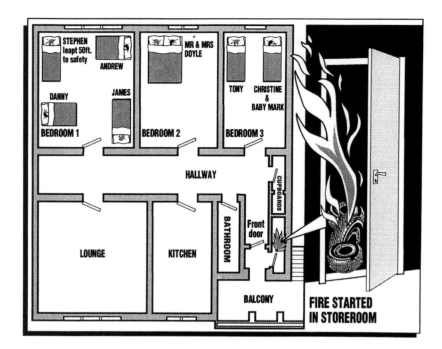

Labels within graphic:
STEPHEN leapt 50ft. to safety
ANDREW
MR & MRS DOYLE
TONY
CHRISTINE & BABY MARK
DANNY
JAMES
BEDROOM 1
BEDROOM 2
BEDROOM 3
HALLWAY
CUPBOARDS
BATHROOM
Front door
LOUNGE
KITCHEN
BALCONY
FIRE STARTED IN STOREROOM

This newspaper graphic shows the layout of the Doyle flat. The blaze started in a storeroom but burst through the house with explosive speed. For some there was no escape.

plotting to build up an ice-cream business by threats and intimidation. After this, there were more arrests related to the Bankend Street blaze. But, in the end, after a trial lasting almost a month, Campbell and Steele were convicted of the murder of the Doyles. Both were given life sentences for the fire attack.

From day one of their conviction, Campbell and Steele swore their innocence. Campbell claimed that the police knew he was not responsible and that they had charged him in order to force him to reveal the identity of the real culprit. This, he said, he could not do as he did not know who was responsible. There followed years of headlines as Campbell and Steele carried out stunts and protests to keep their case before the public. They steadfastly denied guilt, refusing parole and staging hunger strikes and spectacular breaks for freedom. On one occasion, they were freed to await a court hearing and then re-incarcerated.

Their convictions were finally quashed at the Court of Appeal in March 2004. There had always been concern from the start of the investigation about some of the actions of the police but, after so many years, that all seemed pretty much to be water under the bridge – until the emergence of an expert witness, Professor Brian Clifford, a London psychologist, at the final appeal. Detectives at the trial, back in the eighties, insisted that Steele and Campbell had made incriminating statements. Campbell was supposed to have said, 'The fire at the Fat Boy's (Andrew Doyle's) was only meant to be a frightener that went too far.' He was adamant that he had never said that but the claim was recorded in the notebooks of four officers. Professor Clifford did some investigating and research and his results made it clear that it was extremely unlikely that four officers would separately record what was said in such similar terms as they did.

Inside the ambulance taking members of the Doyle family away from the scene are a fireman, on the left, Andrew Doyle in the middle and Daniel Doyle. Andrew died but, despite his extensive burns, Daniel survived.

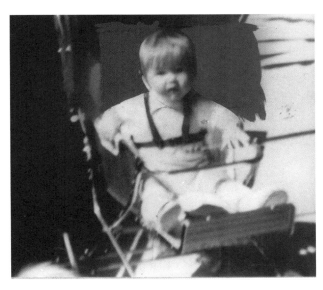

This is Mark Doyle, the youngest victim of the Bankend Street fire.

The slaughter of six members of the Doyle family in the Ice-Cream Wars of the eighties shocked the city. Thousands lined the streets to pay their respects as the funeral cortege drove by.

The scale of the Bankend Street tragedy is emphasised as the coffins of the victims are lined up. Hundreds of mourners waited outside.

It convinced the judge at the appeal who said:

> Our conclusion is that any jury hearing Professor Clifford's evidence would have assessed the evidence of the arresting officers in an entirely different light. The evidence of Professor Clifford is of such significance that the verdicts of the jury, having been returned in ignorance of it, must be regarded as miscarriages of justice.

The Glasgow two were free at last. Who did kill the Doyles? Underworld rumours there are aplenty but no facts.

While Campbell and Steele were thumbing through law books and dreaming up new stunts, all was, of course, not quiet in the streets. In the underworld, two names dominated the final years of the twentieth century in this turbulent city – Paul Ferris and Tam McGraw. Ferris was cleared of killing Arthur Thompson Jr but later jailed for gunrunning. He returned, after a long prison sentence, claiming to be a reformed character. McGraw, too, always a sinister figure, ended up in court, accused of bankrolling a major drug-running operation but 'walked' as they say on the streets. His not proven verdict came after a fifty-five-day trial and he left the court telling reporters to 'f★★★ off' before sweeping away in style in his black Mercedes. Their spectacular trials apart, McGraw and Ferris continued to make headlines day after day as the tabloids reported on the current happenings in gangland Glasgow.

Despite the efforts of gangbusters galore, it has to be faced that the gangs are not bust, even in the twenty-first century. In their declining days, the two infamous old Glasgow Godfathers, Walter Norval and Arthur Thompson, had to watch the bloody rise of their successors. It will happen again, no matter how hard the city polishes its new reputation. There is no shortage of evil wannabes lurking in the shadows, ready to run the drugs and fight for their turf. They are there. We don't know their names but we will, we will.

Both TC Campbell and Joe Steele were driven to try to get their verdicts overturned. They used every means to keep the injustice in the public eye. TC went on hunger strike and was often at odds with prison authorities. Steele, on one occasion, escaped and fled to London to tell the press his side of the story. Other stunts involved Steele climbing this surveillance tower outside Barlinnie. He also glued himself to the railings of Buckingham Palace.

Here is TC Campbell, right, with his brother-in-law Thomas Lafferty, a heavy-drinking loose cannon of the underworld. He was known as 'The Shadow' as he was never far from Campbell's side. Before the fatal fire, Lafferty and Campbell had been accused of attacking Andrew Doyle's ice-cream van.

This is TC in the Bar-L during the long years of fighting to prove his innocence and that of Joe Steele.

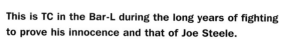

Both men aged considerably in prison. Here they are briefly on the outside in 1992 (TC is on the right).

By the early nineties, the pressure to release Steele and Campbell was building up. Joe Steele's young nephew was among this banner-waving group. Away from the streets, Steele's lawyer and some high-profile journalists were working to overturn the wrongful verdict handed down to 'The Glasgow Two'.

Underworld funerals often feature in Glasgow newspaper files. This was the scene as the coffin of Billy McPhee arrived at Daldowie crematorium in May 2003. A henchman of the so-called 'Licensee', Tam McGraw, McPhee was stabbed to death in full view of customers in a Baillieston pub/restaurant. Anyone there to eat, drink and watch sport on the big-screen TV got more than they bargained for. Mark Clinton was accused of the killing but, with his trial barely started, he was cleared in court when the Crown Prosecutor announced that the indictment was being withdrawn because crucial evidence from two eyewitnesses was insufficient for the case to go ahead. Clinton had lodged special defences – one claiming he was elsewhere at the time and the other blaming three other men.

Paul Ferris is perhaps the most public face of the modern crop of gangsters. Cleared of the murder of Fatboy Thompson, he does a classic 'walk to freedom' on the steps of High Court. Two years later, he was sent down at the Old Bailey for gunrunning. He emerged from prison in the south claiming to be a reformed character.

In this shot Ferris is without the smart suit, collar and tie, a uniform he likes almost as much as his old associate Arthur Thompson Sr did.

High-flying legal eagles are a Glasgow speciality and it seems there is never a shortage of villains to keep the top lawyers in headlines and cash. Donald Findlay is the latest in a memorable collection of pleaders, declaiming the innocence of his clients with the masterly style of such famous predecessors as Joe Beltrami and Laurence Dowdall.

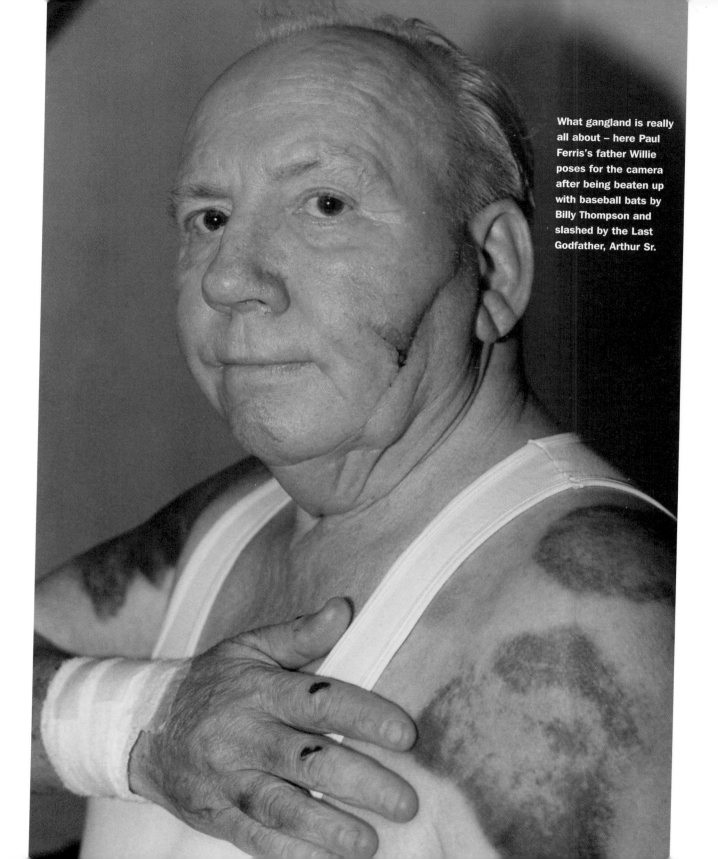

What gangland is really all about – here Paul Ferris's father Willie poses for the camera after being beaten up with baseball bats by Billy Thompson and slashed by the Last Godfather, Arthur Sr.

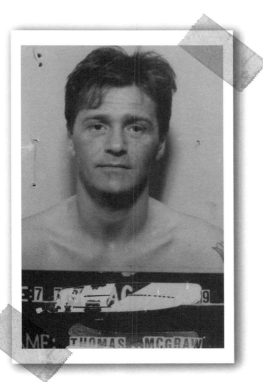

Here is Tam 'The Licensee' McGraw as a young man looking his hardest. In his early days, he worked as an enforcer for the Barlanark Team. His look changed over the years and now, when photographed, he tends to wear a smart suit and favours the style of the retired businessman. His time in gangland has made him immensely rich but it has also brought him battles with the taxman as well as battles on the streets. At one stage, he was reported to be worth £20 million, with homes in Mount Vernon and under the Spanish sun.

Man of the Clyde George Parsonage Sr, of the Glasgow Humane Society, spent many years saving lives on the river and pulling bodies from its murky waters – sometimes they were the victims of a crime, sometimes victims of an accident or suicide. On his retirement, his son took over from him.

For many Glaswegians, HMP Barlinnie is merely a gaunt fortress glimpsed from cars or buses speeding past on the M8 but there is always time to speculate what it might be like in this place where some spent years wasting away and others died in the infamous hanging shed. Hardened criminals, much used to the place, saw it differently. The city's original Godfather, Walter Norval, took delight in singing the following little song to me:

BARLINNIE HOTEL
In Glasgow's fair city,
There's flashy hotels.
They give board and lodgings
To all the big swells.
But the greatest of all now
Is still in full swing –
Five beautiful mansions,
Controlled by the king.
There's bars on the windows,
And bells on the door,
Dirty big guard beds,
Attached to the floor,
I know 'cause I have been there,
And sure I can tell,
There's no place on earth like
The Barlinnie Hotel.
I was driven from the Sheriff,
And driven by bus,
Drove through the streets,
Like a gangster at state,
And they never slowed up,
Till they got to the gate.
As we entered reception,
They asked my name,
And asked me my address,
And the reason I came.
As I answered these questions,
A screw rang the bell –
It was time for my bath,
In Barlinnie Hotel.
After my bath, I was dressed like a doll.
The screw said, 'Quick march,
Right into E-hall.'
As I entered my flowery,*
I looked round in vain,
To think that three years here
I had to remain.
For breakfast next morning,
I asked for an egg.
The screw must have thought
I was pulling his leg.
For, when he recovered, he let out a yell,
'Jailbirds don't lay eggs,
In the Barlinnie Hotel!'
The day came for me
When I had to depart.
I was as sick as a dog,
With joy in my heart.
For the comfort was good,
And the service was swell,
But I'll never return
To Barlinnie Hotel!

* Slang for cell

Nice song, shame about the ending. For one thing is sure – Barlinnie, as long as it stands, will never be short of customers and many of them will be repeat business.

Index